# I FISHED MY WAY THROUGH LIFE

John Lesterson

# I FISHED MY WAY THROUGH LIFE

### THE WILD LIFE STORY OF
### A RETIRED ALASKAN FISHING GUIDE!

John Lesterson

PO Box 221974 Anchorage, Alaska 99522-1974
books@publicationconsultants.com, www.publicationconsultants.com

ISBN Number: 978-1-59433-879-3
eBook ISBN Number: 978-1-59433-880-9
Library of Congress Catalog Card Number: 2019905874

Copyright 2019 John Lesterson
—First Edition—

All rights reserved, including the right of reproduction in any form, or by any mechanical or electronic means including photocopying or recording, or by any information storage or retrieval system, in whole or in part in any form, and in any case not without the written permission of the author and publisher.

Manufactured in the United States of America

# Table of Contents

Introduction..................................................................................................7

| Chapter 1 | The making of a fisherman..............................................9 |
| Chapter 2 | The US Army brings me to Alaska ...............................17 |
| Chapter 3 | My new life on my own in Alaska..................................21 |
| Chapter 4 | Tough times ahead and the value of friends ..................27 |
| Chapter 5 | The beginning of a career ...............................................31 |
| Chapter 6 | Smooth sailing ahead .....................................................37 |
| Chapter 7 | Making changes ..............................................................41 |
| Chapter 8 | Hawaii bound .................................................................47 |
| Chapter 9 | Still growing the business and Dawn starts one............53 |
| Chapter 10 | Avalanche........................................................................61 |
| Chapter 11 | Building our first house..................................................67 |
| Chapter 12 | The Kasilof fish camp....................................................71 |
| Chapter 13 | Fish Politics and Burning Out......................................75 |
| Chapter 14 | Saying goodbye ..............................................................79 |
| Chapter 15 | Building our next house................................................93 |

| | | |
|---|---|---|
| Chapter 16 | Hunting | 97 |
| Chapter 17 | The Badger | 103 |
| Chapter 18 | My thoughts and opinions | 107 |
| Chapter 19 | Conclusion | 117 |

# Introduction

I have always enjoyed reading books about people's lives, especially about the early pioneers of Alaska. If it had anything to do with fishing, hunting or survival it was all the better. Over time I have come to realize that my life has been an incredible journey. I lived my life by my rules and my rules only for the most part. I have had many people over the years tell me that I should write a book about my life story. I'm not sure if I want to call it a mid life crises or ego trip or whatever, but I figured screw it, I'm going to do it.

When I started this book I thought it was going to be easy. Man was I ever in for an education. This was one of the

Life and fishing are very similar. You never know what's at the end of the line. That's what makes it so truly good.

more difficult things I have ever done in my life and it was also very rewarding. I was surprised at when I started this how my memory brought back so many things that I had totally forgotten about. As I wrote this there were times I cried like a little baby and there were times I laughed my ass off. I put it all out there for you to read. There's no bullshit in this book. This is my life.

I dedicate this book in memory of my dad who gave me so much and taught me how to fish, and to my mother for putting up with all my crap when I was a kid. I further want to dedicate this book to my wife Dawn, the true love of my life, for putting up with me for the last 33 years. Without you I doubt that this book would have ever been written. And to my grandkids, I hope you have as much fun and opportunity in your life as I did.

I thank my sister Kelli, my hunting and fishing partner Gene Dyson, my old deck hand Matt Blattmachr and my sweet dear friend Laurie Wood for reading this and giving me their input.

I truly hope you enjoy reading this book as much as I had writing it.

*John Lesterson*

CHAPTER 1

# The making of a fisherman

As long as I can remember, I've had a love for fishing. When I was four years old, my mother married my stepfather Alex, who lucky for me loved to fish. At the time he was in the Air Force stationed in upstate Michigan where I was born. Since I was going to be an Air Force brat I was going to be able to travel, live and fish in many different places. At the age of five, our family moved to Bermuda where we would spend the next three years. I can remember walking on the reefs with my dad fishing for barracuda. I knew then that I wanted to be a fisherman. When we would go diving, we would see all these fish and all I could think about was how could I catch them. When I started school all I could think about was getting back to the water. I flunked the first grade. The teacher wrote on my report card that I had no interest in learning anything. This was the beginning of a long not so good school habits that must have been a nightmare for my parents.

In 1965 our family moved to Denver where we would spend the next five years. It was during this time I would learn to fish for trout and many other kinds of freshwater fish. I would also get my first education in ice fishing, which is something I still cherish today.

I can remember peddling my bicycle eight miles out of Denver into the country to a lake called Cheery creek reservoir, which is now surrounded by Denver. I would catch so many fish there that I would have a stringer of fish wrapped around my handlebars. I would have fish in my coat pockets, pants pockets or anywhere else I could put them. I would have trout, catfish, perch or anything else I could catch. In my eyes, a fish was a fish. I remember my dad having to come look for me because I was late getting home. Way late. However, he couldn't scold me to bad. After all, I was just fishing, and he too was a fisherman.

Our first winter in Denver and every winter afterward my dad would take me ice fishing for trout all over Colorado.

My dad and I living the dream.

I loved it. Give me an ice auger, fishing pole and bait and I would stay out all day. I remember one year my dad was going on an ice fishing trip over the Christmas holiday. This was back when Santa Clause was still an important person in my life. It was my choice, stay home for Santa or go ice fish with dad. I chose ice fishing.

One of the conditions for ice fishing with dad was I had to clean all the fish. We always stayed in a small camper, so I would have to clean the fish out on the frozen lake. If the fish weren't clean enough, my dad would make me go back out and wash them again. I remember my hands were freezing cold from washing off the fish in the ice cold water. I loved it. I loved catching them, cleaning them and eating them.

In the summer my dad would take his thirty-day leave from the service and our family would drive across the USA, from Montana where we had relatives too Michigan where we also had family. We always stayed at KOA campgrounds that had fishing close by. As a kid, I was able to fish across the USA for several different kinds of fish. How lucky could a kid be?

One summer I was lucky enough to spend a month with my Aunt and Uncle in Livingston, Montana. My Uncle worked for the railroad, had a team of horses and loved to fish and hunt. My Aunt tied flies for Dan Bailey's fly shop, which is a very famous fly fishing store in Montana. She did this for twenty-five years and was a master of the art. I remember watching my Aunt tying flies at her desk. She was good at it. I was fascinated by the way she could tie a fly so fast. I knew then I was soon going to be tying my own flies and learning the art of fly fishing. My Aunt would give my cousins and me a hand full of flies and off we would go on our bicycles to fish the Yellowstone River for rainbow and brown trout. We use to catch and keep lots of fish - big ones, little ones, it didn't matter. I believe the limit was ten back then. It is kind of funny now because most trout fishing is catch and release and for a good reason.

My Uncle would take my cousins and me up into the mountains by horseback to fly fish for cutthroat trout. It was beautiful, fishing in lakes full of fish surrounded by pristine wilderness and no other people. Little did I know that several years later I would have the pleasure of taking my Uncle fishing in my playground in Alaska. Life was pretty good for a boy who was not even a teenager yet.

In 1970 our family moved to San Antonio, Texas where my dad would finish his career in the Air Force. This is where things get interesting. I was becoming a teenager, looking at girls a little differently but more importantly, I was living in bass and catfish country. I always had dreams of catching big bass, so Texas was just fine for me.

Every chance I had I would hike back into ponds and lakes and fish for bass, catfish or anything else I could catch. What makes this more different than before is that in Texas almost all the land is private. This means that I would have to sneak into all these places to fish, and I must say the fishing was good. In Texas, it was a serious offense for trespassing. Because of this, my dad couldn't fish with me. Catching a kid on a private pond was much different than catching an adult. After all, what could they do to a kid for just fishing? I would soon find out. I got caught twice in two different places. Both times they took my fishing pole, tackle, and all my fish and told me never to come back. In Texas, they just do not want you on their land. This wouldn't stop me.

One night a school buddy and I went fishing at one of our favorite ponds. On this pond, the landowner had a small boat that he would use to pull his trout lines. We decided we would use the boat that night. We tried to be as quiet as possible while we were fishing, but a dog heard us and started barking. On came the outside lights at the house and out came the owner with a gun, which is common in Texas. Now we are paddling as fast as we could to get to shore. Once we got to land, we pushed the boat back out into the pond to make it more difficult for the owner to retrieve it. We figured this would teach him for not allowing us to fish on his pond. As we were running away, I realized one thing. I had left my tackle box in the boat. The owner not only got my tackle box he got the last laugh.

My first year in the eighth grade, notice I say the first year, was a good one for me and not so good for my mom and dad. On the way to the school bus stop in the mornings, I would meet my school buddy and off we would go through the woods to fish our favorite lakes. I kept my fishing tackle hidden in the woods so that my parents wouldn't know what I was up to. We fished almost daily.

Since both my mom and dad worked I was able to get home and get the mail first. I was able to sort out the letters from school telling them that I was not passing and missing lots of classes. The report cards were computer printed and also mailed. With a number two pencil, I was able to take an F and turn it into a B. My parents were so proud of me. I was finally doing well in school. They were buying me gifts, increased my allowance, and my dad would take me fishing on weekends to places like Rockport for saltwater fishing, the Rio Grande and all over south Texas. Little did they know that I was bass fishing almost every week.

When the school year was over my dad took my school buddy and me up to a lake where we always dreamed of fishing for big bass and catfish. He gave us money for bait and food and left us for a week. It was our reward for doing so well in school. When he came back to pick us up the party was over. Our gig was up. I think at that point my parents were giving up with me. It must have been a heartbreaker for them to learn that not only was I not doing well in school I wasn't even going to school. All I could say was, "I may not know algebra, but I am a better fisherman than any kid in school." That was the only thing important to me.

For the few years we spent in Texas I learned a lot about fishing, catching snakes and turtles and all the things a boy would have fun doing. In the summers we would still spend a month driving across the USA camping and of course fishing. For all the fun things I did, there was a new place I was starting to dream of - Alaska. When I would watch a TV show about Alaska with all the salmon and bears, I would tell myself that when I grow up, I am going to Alaska.

In the spring of 1973, our family moved to Great Falls, Montana. My dad was stationed there in 1957, and it was his dream that someday he would go back to Montana and live. Now that he was retired with the Air Force it was time for his dream to come true. Montana was going to be a new experience for me because now I would be living in the center of fishing paradise.

On our first day in Great Falls, I walked down to the Missouri river and met an old man fishing on the river. His name was Charlie. This was the beginning of a good friendship. I didn't know I just met a man who was a world war two veteran, was born and raised in Montana and fished almost every day. The next day I walked back down to the river with my fishing pole, and there was Charlie. He had a couple of trout on a stringer. I hooked a trout and yelled to Charlie "I got one," and he yelled back at me and said: "you don't have him till he's in the net." I lost that fish. I will always remember Charlie's words.

Within a few weeks, Charlie started to take me fishing with him. Since he was raised in northern Montana, he knew where all the best fishing was, private or public. He knew all the back roads. In every small town we would come to, Charlie knew the people. Ranchers, farmers, bartenders, everyone knew Charlie, even the game wardens. You see Charlie believed the limit was when you ran out of bait, or the fish quit biting, whichever came first. It sounded good to me. As the summer went on, I fished all over northern Montana. I fished for trout, northern pike, walleyes or whatever I could get my hands on. The fishing was great. I got to meet the landowners who controlled the access. What a summer it was, all this from simply meeting an old man on the river my first day in Great Falls.

During our first winter in Great Falls, I would spend most of my weekend's ice fishing with old man Charlie or my dad. Unfortunately, my dad had to work most of the time, so he couldn't join me. I remember ice fishing in temperatures well below zero, and within thirty minutes it would be forty above. These were the Chinook winds that Montana was famous for. You had to be there to believe it.

I did so poorly in Texas schools that when it was time for school to start my parents decided to put me in Our Lady of Lords, a private Catholic School. The one thing I can say about a Catholic school is if you don't pass you will be punished. In my typing class, one of our assignments was to make a book. The book I made was called everything you wanted to know about fishing but was afraid to ask. I believe I had the highest grade in the class and it was the best grade I ever received in school. I guess this was a sign of what was to be.

Because the Catholic school only went to the ninth grade, the following year I went to Great Falls High. Ah yes, back to public school. No more getting my ear pulled by the sweet little nun for screwing up. What makes this even better is that now I was old enough to drive and I had a car with my fishing tackle in the trunk. On the way to school, I would somehow make a wrong turn and end up at one of my favorite fishing spots. I did, however, attend school most of the time. After my stunt in the eighth grade, my parents were watching me a little closer.

One of the mandatory classes in the tenth grade was local history. That meant studying the Lewis and Clark expedition. I loved it. I only wish I could have been on it. I think that was the only class that I received credit in that year. I flunked everything else. I don't think my parents were too impressed.

The following spring my mother was diagnosed with breast cancer. Our family was turned upside down. Back then the survival rate for this cancer wasn't good. When my dad would come home from work, we would go fish a small private lake outside of town before we would go visit mom in the hospital. We did this every day. Sometimes we would only fish for an hour or so. I think my dad needed this as bad as I did. I'm always amazed how fishing can make you forget about your troubles and all the screwed-up crap that a person can encounter in your life.

When my mother came home from the hospital, she asked us kids if we wanted to be adopted by dad or go back to Michigan and live with our birth father if she didn't make it. Those must have been hard words for my mom to ask. I don't know what my brother and sister answered, but I choose to be adopted. After all, my dad was my fishing partner. Fortunately, forty-five years later my mother is alive and well, cancer free.

That summer I continued to fish all over Montana. I always carried a five-gallon gas can and a siphoning hose. If I didn't have enough money for gas, I would just simply go steal some. I'm not proud of that now, but at least I was just stealing gas. These days the kids would rather steal the vehicle. I think if I ever catch a kid stealing gas from me so he or she can go fishing I will just simply take them to the gas station and fill their tank.

When it was time for school to start I went for three days of my junior year. I decided that there was nothing more I was going to learn in school that was going to help me in life. After all, my sophomore year was my twelfth year in school. When my parents found out that I wasn't going to school my mother pulled me aside and gave me the ultimatum - either go back to school, get a job or get out. Those were the best words my mother could have ever given me.

CHAPTER 2

# THE US ARMY BRINGS ME TO ALASKA

Since I was only seventeen, I asked my mother that if I were to join the military would she sign the papers. She was more than happy to do so. I think she wanted me out. When I went to talk to the army recruiter, I asked him if there was any way I could get to Alaska if I were to join. He told me if I would join combat arms [infantry] I could get to Alaska. I told him to sign me up. My dream was finally starting to come true. I am finally going to Alaska. In October 1975 I said goodbye to my family, boarded a plane to Fort Knox, Kentucky to start my military tour.

Ah yes, welcome to the U.S. Army. After spending six weeks of basic training at Fort Knox, Kentucky, the army sent me to Fort Polk, Louisiana, where I would spend another two months doing combat training. Now there is a lake close by called Toledo Bend reservoir, which sits on the Texas and Louisiana border. As a kid, I had always dreamed of fishing this lake. It didn't take me long to make friends with a guy who had a car and enjoyed fishing. We found a place where we could rent a cabin and a boat for fifteen dollars a day. I spent every weekend for the next two months fishing for bass, and I must say the fishing was outstanding. I was starting to think that this Army stuff is ok.

Now the Army gives me my orders to go to Alaska. My dream is finally coming true. I was sent to Fort Wainwright in Fairbanks. A military van picked me up at the airport. On the way back to the base I spotted a moose along the road. There was lots of snow on the ground, and it was cold. I loved it. I knew then that this is the place for me. Just before we arrived on base, I see the road sign (North Pole 10 miles). Not knowing that there was a town called the North Pole outside of Fairbanks I just thought they really sent me up here. Within a month I was sent to Fort Richardson in Anchorage for three months of mechanics school. During this time, I found myself ice fishing all over south-central Alaska. Once again, this Army stuff is ok. When I returned to Fairbanks, I was assigned a jeep since I am now a mechanic. Now, this is where the fun begins.

My sergeant and I were pretty good buddies. He also had a jeep assigned to him and liked to fish. We would go to the Auto shop in the mornings and work on our jeeps. Maybe we would adjust our brakes or some other minor thing. Of course, after we would work on our jeeps, now we must test drive them to make sure we did the work properly. This means going into the backwoods of Fort Wainwright where we just so happened to have our fishing tackle stashed. We would fish all day, go back to the auto shop to return the jeeps and go back to our platoon to get off work at five o'clock. We did this all summer. Now, this Army stuff is way too easy. Our officer knew we were up to something, but he could never figure it out. I loved it. I guess it was my first experience with getting paid to fish.

One of my more enjoyable times in the Army was when we were flown in on a mountain and glacier training exercise in the Alaska mountain range. We would repel down into the glacier and see nothing but blue ice as far down as you could see. Then we would climb mountains as high as we could get. The entire battalion camped on the glacier for a week. The Dahl sheep would come right up to the glacier and check us out. Big trophy Rams and lots of them. It was truly an incredible sight. At the end of the week, the entire battalion walked out to Fort Greely. A twenty-five-mile walk I might add. Well, five hundred guys walking twenty-five miles makes for a heck of good trail and this area is a non-motorized area for hunting and sheep season was coming up.

When we returned to Fort Wainwright, the Army had the bright idea that all high school dropouts go to a GED school, which was about what seemed like half the Army. Now is this just great or what. I'm going back to school with sheep season coming on. The third day in this class the teacher was up at the chalkboard saying something about X Times Y equals whatever or some crap like that which to this day I don't know what it means and could really care less. I thought to myself I don't need this crap. This is why I'm in the Army anyway, to get out of school. We had a new company commander who just so happened to like fishing and hunting. I went and requested permission to drop out of the class and two weeks leave to go sheep hunting. He granted it. I couldn't believe it. Ha, now I'm a double dropout which I have no regrets.

My sergeant who fished with me all summer and I took our leave and walked back to the glacier where we were just at a few weeks earlier. We both shot a sheep and had a great time. There was a creek up there that was so full of Grayling all you had to do was shoot into it, and a few would come floating up from the concussion of the bullet. Fresh fish without a fishing pole, now life is good. When we returned to Fort Wainwright, our company commander called me to his office. All I could think was what possibly could I have done this time. When I arrived at his office, gave a salute and he tells me to grab a seat. Then he asks, "how was the hunt"? This guy was great, and we remained friends for the rest of my military time.

Throughout my two years in the Army, I did plenty of fishing and plenty of growing up. I didn't like the Army, and I'm sure the Army did not like me. I have great respect for the men and women in the armed forces. It's not a job for everyone. All I can say is thank you, Uncle Sam; you got me to Alaska. I have no regrets.

CHAPTER 3

# My new life on my own in Alaska

On October 19th, 1977 I received my honorable discharge from the Army. The day I got out they gave me five hundred and four dollars. This was for my leave I had accumulated and a plane ticket back to Montana. I was nineteen years old and on my own for the first time. No place to live and no one to feed me. It was either go back to Montana and live with my family or stay and try to make it in Alaska. I chose to stay. I hitchhiked around Fairbanks, found a small efficiency apartment for four hundred dollars a month. I told the landlord that I just got out of the Army, so he didn't charge me for a deposit. I went to the store and bought fifty dollars' worth of food. I had fifty-four dollars left in my pocket. Within three days I had a job. I hitchhiked back and forth to work each day until I was able to save enough money to buy a car. I would like to say that most of the time I was hitchhiking the temperature was well below zero or close to it.

I say all this because I want you to know how bad I wanted to make it in Alaska and the hardships I was willing to endure. When I hear people say they can't make it or people on welfare crying about how hard life is, I must laugh. They can go screw themselves. There singing the blues to the wrong person. If there was one thing I learned in the Army, there is nothing you can't do if you want it bad enough or have no choice.

Fairbanks was rocking at this time. Everyone was young and full of money from the pipeline construction. It was basically working all day and party all night. I was right in the middle of it. After my first six months of working, I took two weeks off and went back to Montana. My family thought I was moving back. Why else would a twenty-year-old be coming home? For most of the two weeks, I spent fishing with my dad at all our old fishing spots. It was the first-time fishing with my dad as an adult. We both had a great time.

When it was time to leave I told my family at the airport that if they ever wanted to see me again, they would have to come to Alaska to do so as I was never coming back. I think they knew then that I was serious. Four months later I get a phone call at work from my dad. He said they were in Tok junction and would be in Fairbanks by the end of the day. They sold everything in Montana and were moving to Anchorage without ever seeing Alaska. I had to laugh with joy. With all the hell I put my parents through growing up being a fishing bum they were now following me. Once they got settled in Anchorage, my dad told me he wished he would have listened to me years earlier and moved up here. He loved it.

For all the fun I had in Fairbanks and all the good people I had the pleasure to meet, I figured there must be someplace better or at least someplace warmer in Alaska to live. The economy was crashing as the pipeline construction had now been over for a year. Since I had been spending my money like a drunken sailor chasing women all over Fairbanks, I was now broke. It was time to move. I figured I would go to Anchorage, get a job, save some money and decide where I wanted to move to. The day I left Fairbanks the temperature was almost sixty below. I knew where ever I was going to move to; it was going to be warmer.

As I made my way to Anchorage, the temperature was above zero. I figured this was more like it. It only took a few months to realize that this town wasn't for me. I guess I just don't like the big city. I left Anchorage and headed for Homer on the southern part of the Kenai Peninsula. The place was beautiful. The weather was much warmer than Fairbanks, and it was a peninsula surrounded by the ocean with mountains. This was the place for me.

On my first day in town, I drove out to what is known as the homer spit. This is a four-mile point of land that reaches out into Kachemak Bay. There were several small boats fishing just offshore. I wondered what these people could be fishing for. It was King Crab. Great big King Crab and plenty of them and catching them with fishing rods out of all crazy things. It only took a few days to make friends with a guy who owned a boat, and I was eating King Crab. Now life is good.

I pitched a tent on the Homer spit where I would spend the next couple months. My parents eventually loaned me there motor home to stay in. I got a job at a cannery processing crab. My goal was to become a commercial fisherman on a crab boat. A person could make lots of money on a crab boat. I guess it goes to show you how dumb I was back then, trying to get one of the most dangerous jobs in Alaska.

One night while sitting in the bar drinking beer, a friend came in and asked me if I wanted to go commercial crabbing that night. Now was my chance. I am finally going to be a crab fisherman. We headed out across Kachemak Bay to pull pots and move them up in the bay. The weather was cold and windy. After pulling what seemed like hundreds of pots, we started to head up in the bay when suddenly bells and whistles were going off, and there was smoke coming from the engine compartment.

The captain, who was a farmer from Oregon, begins to panic. We opened the engine hatch and found it to be full of what looked like water up to the engine. The captain thinks we're sinking and wants to start the engine and head for land. At this point, I was ready to start throwing crab pots off the boat or anything else to keep the boat floating. That should tell you how much I knew. My friend jumps down into the engine compartment and yells at the captain not to start the engine. It wasn't water. It was the fuel that had been leaking from one of the fuel lines while the engine was running. We had to call the Coast Guard to come rescue us. Everyone had agreed that had the captain started the boat to head back the boat would have probably caught fire, and instead of writing this book I would have been crab bait. This was my first and only experience as a commercial fisherman, and it scared the crap out of me. My friend, who asked me to go out that night, eventually landed a job on a King Crab boat on the Bering Sea. I heard later that he was washed overboard and never found.

For the next few months in Homer, I helped build a charter office for one of the first Halibut fishing business in Homer. I had no idea then that Homer was going to become the Halibut fishing capital of the world. There must be well over one hundred fishing charters there now.

I decided to move to Soldotna my first summer on the Kenai Peninsula. I had met a few people from there, and they told me about the fishing on the Kenai and Kasilof rivers. This would be the first time that I would see tens of thousands of salmon in a river. It was an incredible sight. There were so many fish back then and so few people fishing.

I had a friend who lived on the Kenai river with great red fishing in his front yard. I also new a commercial fisherman who would sell our fish on his fish ticket for twenty cents a pound. I think our best night we made almost fifteen hundred dollars. Not bad for just snagging fish with a fishing pole. I made enough money off the red run to pay my rent for the first year. Now life is good.

There were only one or two fishing guides on the Kenai River and no one on the Kasilof River at that time. Now there are over three hundred. Back then no one had any idea that the charter industry was going to grow the way it did and how it was going to change the Kenai and Kasilof Rivers as well as many other places on the Kenai Peninsula for the good or bad, depending on whom you talk to.

My first job in Soldotna was pumping gas for Soldotna sales and service. While I was working there, I was trying to get a job in the oil industry. After all, that was where the big money was. The owner of the gas station, the late John Ingram, pulled me aside one day and told me "buddy if you want to get somewhere in this town this is the best job you can have. Pump their gas and meet the people." That was the best piece of advice anyone could have told me.

I met the man who owned a roofing company who would eventually hire me and teach me the trade of roofing and construction in general. I also met the folks that would eventually help me start my fishing business.

That job pumping gas for five bucks an hour ended up being the best job I ever had.

The following year I started my first business, JKL seafood. The JKL is the initials to my full name. I was going to Homer, buying Crab and Shrimp and selling it back in Soldotna. I could double my money fast. If I took them to Fairbanks, I could triple my money, which I did quite often. My record run to Fairbanks consisted of eight thousand pounds of Halibut, and I sold it in less than three days. I did well with it until I decided that snorting cocaine and chasing women was more important than making money. I was young and dumb.

In the spring of 81, a friend asked me if I wanted to go to Bristol Bay to be a herring spotter. If you think I was dumb trying to get a job on a crab boat, this was even dumber. You see the fishing boats can't see the herring from the water. They need an airplane to spot them and direct them to the fish. Plenty of fish in one area means plenty of planes in one area. My job was to make sure we were holding our altitude and watch for other planes as midair collisions were common in this fishery.

In the three weeks I was there we flew eighty-eight hours up and down the Bristol Bay coast and Norton Sound. I had the pleasure to meet the Eskimo people of the region and how they lived. I didn't make very much money on this journey, but the experience was worth its weight in gold.

In the mid 70s the state started a hatchery run of King Salmon on the Kasilof River. By the late 70s and early 80s the King Salmon fishing was incredible. Kings by the thousands and very few people. It was almost a well kept secret until they put it on TV one day. This became my dad's favorite place to fish. It was hard to get him away from it.

Throughout the next few years, I worked just enough to get by on and spent most of my time fishing. In the summer months, my dad would travel down from Anchorage to salmon fish with me. Some days he would just fly down for the day. There were a few more Kenai river guides showing up and no one on the Kasilof yet and tourism was just getting started. My dad would say to me at times "you should become a fishing guide." I never really thought much of it, but it did sound kind of good making money for just going fishing.

CHAPTER 4

# Tough times ahead and the value of friends

In the spring of 83, my dad and I had planned a fishing trip with his brother Uncle Max and his son Steven. My dad and Max were very close to each other from the time they were young boys. This would be the first trip to Alaska for Max, and my dad was very excited for it. Our fishing trip was planned for July, in the Iliamna region, which has some of the finest salmon fishing in the world.

In May of that summer, my parents received a phone call from Max. His wife Aunt Carroll had just died of a massive heart attack. Now life has just been turned upside down for Max and Steven. A man who just lost his wife of thirty years and a teenage boy who just lost his mother must have really hurt. Life is not always kind. However, the fishing trip is still a go.

In early June my dad came down from Anchorage to fish the Kasilof River with me, his favorite place. He was very sick and you could see something was wrong. A few of my friends and I got together and took him down to fish our favorite spot. There were probably thirty or forty people fishing as word was out about the fishing. My dad immediately hooks a King in the back, brings it in and keeps it. You could hear a few people mumbling up and down the bank since it was illegal to keep a snagged fish. He then goes back to fishing and catches and keeps two more which is really illegal since the limit was one. Now you could really hear the people mumbling up and down the river. I told my dad its time we get the hell out of here while we can. I think my dad knew there was something wrong with his health and didn't give a shit about getting a ticket. I had no idea that day would be the last time I would ever fish with him.

A week or so later I received a phone call from my mother. She tells me my dad is in the hospital and has been diagnosed with terminal bone cancer. Talk about a sucker punch to the heart. My dad was so weak that he could hardly walk. The doctors told him he was going to die soon, but that chemotherapy could possibly give him an extra month and maybe even a year to live. They also told him the chemo could kill him. I think all he wanted to do was to live long enough to go on our July fishing trip with Max. It was his only chance but, it didn't work. The next day the doctors took him off chemotherapy putting him in a drug-induced coma. Now it was only a matter of time before he would die.

This is where the story gets strange. He wouldn't die. He would wake up from his coma from time to time and start screaming the name, Max. You could hear it all through the floor at the hospital. How my mother had the strength to sit in his room and hold his hand through all this, I don't know. I'm not sure if he could hear us, but all we could do was tell him that Max was on the way. During this time, I also convinced my mom that we should have him buried in Kasilof instead of the military base in Anchorage since he was an old fisherman more than an old soldier and he loved to fish the Kasilof River.

We had called Max and told him to get up here as soon as possible as everything was getting all screwed up. When Max arrived at the airport, I picked him up and probably broke every speed limit to get back to the hospital before it was too late. When we arrived, the doctors gave my dad a drug to wake him up. When he awoke and saw Max, he reached out to him and started yelling his name. It was as if he wanted out of that bed and go on this fishing trip. The doctors immediately gave him drugs to knock him back out. This totally freaked me out. I have never seen anything like it.

The next day on July 3rd Max and I then drove down to Kasilof to buy a plot at the cemetery. When we bought it, I asked them "what about the hole"? They said it was up to us or the mortuary. This is news to me. I said screw it; I will dig the hole myself. We drove back to my place in Soldotna to get a shovel when a friend of mine Dennis Mullican stopped by. When he heard what I was going to do, he grabbed a shovel and joined us. Max was about to find out what kind of friends I have. When we were done digging the hole, we drove back to Soldotna and called my mom at the hospital. She said he just died very peacefully as if he just needed to see Max.

When it came time for the funeral, the Hearse came down from Anchorage and met us in Soldotna. Since the driver didn't know where the cemetery was, he had to follow me. My car was an old Datsun B210 that burned a lot of oil. It was kind of funny; everyone was following the blue smoke to Kasilof. All my friends were there to help and be pallbearers. The VFW came and did the military stuff and gave my mother the flag. When my mother walked away, I grabbed a shovel to fill in the hole, and again Dennis jumped right in and helped me again. We then went back to Soldotna and got drunk. Really drunk!

This probably sounds strange but digging that hole and burying my dad was the most honorable thing I ever did in my life. I was with him to the end, literally. It was the very least I could do for a man that gave me so much.

This was by far the saddest time in my life. I not only lost my dad, but I also lost my best friend and my best fishing buddy. However, my dad taught me a cure for sadness back when my mother was fighting cancer, Fishing and our fishing trip did go on. Max, Steven, my brother and I all went to Iliamna and had a great time. I have been on better fishing trips in my life but never one so badly needed.

To make a long story short over such a sad turn of events, Max and my mother began dating and got married a year later. It was a cool wedding. I cried like a little baby watching my mom get married. They were happily married for twenty-seven years. My mom's last name never even had to change. They spent most of the years in Alaska until Max's health forced them to leave Alaska and move to North Carolina where Max came from. Max died October 31st, 2011. He was a good man who got to live a full life.

In the summer of 84, while working on a roofing project, I stumbled caring a bucket of hot tar. The result was 3rd degree burns up my arm and down my back. I was the first tar burn patient in the Soldotna hospital. I thought to myself, how much more bad luck could I have.

It took eight months for my arm to heal. I had to go to physical therapy three days a week. It was during this time I began to meet tourist in the campgrounds, and I would take them fishing to more secluded areas. Some people would pay me twenty dollars and others would give me a hundred.

Fishing with my mom and Max.

I was just happy to make gas and beer money. I also kept thinking about what my dad had told me about becoming a fishing guide.

I was doing so much fishing that I kept getting fish blood on my bandage. This didn't help the healing of my arm as I kept getting blood poisoning. The doctors and nurses couldn't say too much as I was bringing them fresh fish on a regular basis.

That summer I also moved my old trailer house out to my friend Dennis Mulicans family homestead on Sevena Lake, also known as Soldotna Lake. This place was beautiful. Dennis's mom and dad homesteaded it in the early 60s and it was an honor to be invited out there to live. The lake was full of Northern pike and no people. The nearest neighbor was at least a few miles away. Talk about peace and quite with great fishing and hunting. Wood heat was the only source of heat and no electricity. I loved it.

On April 1st, 1985 my home burned down. I only owned it for a few years and it wasn't much, but it was mine. My dog got me up just in time to get out. I was able to save my guns, fishing poles, some fish pictures and one armload of clothes. Every time I ran back inside, my dog would go back in with me. I lost everything else I owned including the flag that was draped over my dad's casket. That one hurt bad, really bad.

The temperature that night was twelve below. As I stood there watching my place go up in flames, I thought to myself, what next? Within two years my dad died, I burned my arm up, and now I lose everything I own. I talk about all these hardships for one reason. For all the crap one can encounter in your life, you get up and keep walking in the direction you choose. If you have good health and good friends, there's nothing you can't do. After all, this is America.

After my dad died and Max became a part of my immediate family, he was very impressed with the quality and quantity of friends I had. Max looked at me one day and said, "you're stuck with your relatives whether you like it or not and your friends you earn, and you keep them." Man, how true those words are. Now I needed my friends more than ever before.

Throughout the summer of 85, I stayed with several different friends and continued to fish the Kenai and Kasilof rivers. A friend loaned me a boat which enabled me to take enough people fishing to make beer and gas money. During this time, I was drinking far too heavily. I was living for it. I didn't know where I was going or what I was going to do. The one thing I did know is that for the first time in my life I was going nowhere.

Another friend of mine Kearlee Wright, who owned the newly opened Best Western Motel in Soldotna, pulled me aside one day and said, "John sober up this winter and keep your head above ground and I will loan you enough money to buy a boat and refer everyone who needs a guide to you." Kearlee never asked me for anything in return. He just wanted to see me succeed in life. To this day we remain friends, and I consider him to be one of the kindest and sincere men I have ever met in my life.

That fall some friends of mine were having a going away party for a girl who lived in Soldotna and was working in Seattle on a two year contract for the Alaska commercial company. She was here in Alaska for a few days and was getting ready to travel back to Seattle. My friends invited me to the party. I didn't know this girl, but the party sounded good to me. After all, free food and booze, why not? Little did I know then that this girl whose name is Dawn was going to become the love of my life, and my life was going to dramatically change forever.

We began dating soon after meeting each other. Dawn would travel back to Alaska every three weeks or so traveling all over bush Alaska on business. On these trips, she always made it a point to come to Soldotna to see me. For the first time in a few years, I am happy, and my life is finally moving forward instead of backward.

At Christmas time I hawked two of my guns to travel to Seattle to spend the holiday with Dawn and her son Brian. At this time, I knew that I must be falling in love because I don't depart with my guns very easily. I met Dawn's parents on this trip, and her mother asked me what I did for a living. All I could tell her was that I fish. I don't think she was impressed.

Dawn with her mom and dad.

Soon after I returned home Dawn called me and told me she was quitting her job and moving back to Alaska. Her two year contract was up and she wanted to come back and be here with me. I thought to myself what the heck could this girl see in me? All I owned was a few guns, some fishing poles, and an old pickup truck. She, on the other hand, worked her way up the corporate chain to having her own office in Seattle making forty thousand dollars a year which was a lot of money back then and owned a house in Soldotna. All I can say is keep on reading.

CHAPTER 5

# THE BEGINNING OF A CAREER

In March of 86, I flew back to Seattle to help Dawn and Brian pack their belongings for the move back to Alaska. Dawn was really looking forward to moving back to Alaska and doing something new. The plan was she was going to help me with my fishing business, and she was going to go back to school and learn about computers.

Part of our trip back to Alaska was on the state ferry Columbia. This was a three-day trip that took us through the inside passage of Southeast Alaska. The trip was beautiful. It was on this trip that I met a man named Ken Burdett, who would become my first client. Ken was a high ranking military officer who was being transferred to Alaska to be stationed in Anchorage. Ken was also going to be responsible for sending me what seemed like half the military to fish with me. Ken eventually was picked by governer Knowles to become manager of Ted Stevens international.

When we returned to Soldotna, it was time to get serious and start thinking about fishing. I found an old drift boat that some people were selling for one thousand dollars. At the time I didn't have the money. I went to see my friend Kearlee, who had told me several months earlier that he would help me out. Kearlee not only loaned me the money for the boat, but he also gave me an old snowmachine trailer to haul it with.

Kearlee was happy that my life was back on track and he was more than willing to help me succeed.

Kearlee told me one day "if you treat these people good they will come back. These are not poor people that pay you that kind of money to go fishing. If you treat them poorly, you will never see them again". These were some very good words of wisdom. How true it was.

As May approached, I began floating the Kasilof River taking any of my friends who wanted to go. Back then there were no public access points on the river to take a boat out. I had a friend who owned property on the lower river where I was able to take out. It was great. The river was all mine, and the fishing was outstanding. I needed to get the bugs worked out of the boat and get practice for what would be my first real season of guiding. No longer was I going to be taking people fishing for beer and gas money. This was going to be the real deal. I think this was the most excited I have ever been to go fishing in my life.

In the middle of May, I received my first phone call for a guided trip. It was Ken Burdett who I had met on the ferry trip. It was going to be him and one other person. The plan was to fish for King Salmon. We meet the night before at a bar in Soldotna to discuss the next day's fishing trip. As one beer led to another the next thing I knew, we were all too drunk to drive or anything else.

The next morning, I had to walk to the bar to get my truck and get ready for the fishing trip. We had all got so drunk that none of us could remember where we were going to meet. We did finally meet up and went fishing. Let me just say that Dawn was not very impressed. She had just quite a high dollar job to help me start my business, and this is how it starts. It was the first and only time that I ever let alcohol interfere with a fishing charter. For the next sixteen years, I never touched a drop of alcohol on a fishing charter. Now when the charter was done, that was a different story.

Throughout that first summer, I continued to fish almost daily. If I didn't have a charter, I would just simply take friends and family fishing. All I had to do was go catch a King Salmon and take it to a campground where there were tourist and clean it. The tourist would swarm on you like flies. The odds were that one or two of these people were willing to pay you to take them fishing. If they couldn't pay me a hundred dollars, I would charge them fifty. I figured it was better to make fifty dollars than nothing.

That summer I would also see my first of several one-hundred-dollar tips. I knew then that I was good at what I was doing and the people I was taking fishing were more than happy. By the time summer was over my total income was forty-one hundred dollars. Most people would be shocked to have made such a small amount of money. I, on the other hand, was more than pleased, as I knew that this was the beginning of something that had no end in sight.

A man who owned a fishing tackle store in Soldotna offered me a job as a fishing guide for the 87 season. He offered me a thousand dollars a week. Not bad for three or four months of fishing. Most people would have jumped all over it, especially after making such a small amount of money that I did in my first year. I, on the other hand, turned it down. I had enough confidence in myself not to take the job but stay on the course I had chosen. It was the smartest decision I could have made. I knew I was good at what I was doing. Why make someone else look good?

The winter of 86-87 would prove to be quite interesting. It would be the first time that Dawn, Brian and I would spend a full winter together. Since we made such a small amount of money the previous summer, we would need to get jobs. Dawn took on a part-time minimum wage job and went back to school to learn about computers. I took on a job driving a school bus. Out of all the jobs I ever had this was by far the worst. I learned great respect for the people who drive a bus. They have nerves of steel. If I had to drive a bus for more than that year that I did, I would be writing this book from a jail cell serving a life sentence for murder.

When Christmas time came around, with what little money we had saved from fishing, we decided to go to Hawaii. We could only afford to go for a week, so we made the best of it. Instead of staying in Waikiki, renting a motel and doing all the regular tourist crap, we went to the big island of Hawaii, rented a motorhome for fifty bucks a day. We traveled all around the island, camped at several different beaches and met some cool local people. The total cost of our trip minus the airfare was about four hundred bucks. Once again, life is as easy as you want to make it. Little did we not know that this trip to Hawaii was going to be our first of many trips back to the islands.

As springtime was getting closer and fishing season was just around the corner, the most special day in my life happened. On May 16th, 1987, Dawn and I got married. We were perfect for each other. We both left home when we were seventeen and came to Alaska for the adventure and to start new lives. We both loved to fish, camp and everything else Alaska has to offer. We just loved Alaska. Neither of us came here for the money - as so many people working in the oilfield did.

Out of all the things we had in common the greatest thing was that we knew what we wanted in life and we were willing to help each other achieve that. She was helping me with the fishing business working just as hard on the sidelines as I was on the front lines. I was working every side job I could do when I wasn't fishing and learning how to be a father to Brian while she was going to school to learn a new career. Without each other there was very little we could do, and with each other, there was very little we couldn't do. Life is good.

At our wedding, we had everyone from bikers to the bishop of the church as our guests. That shows you the wide variety of friends we had then and still do today. Our honeymoon took us to Homer where we would spend only one night. We didn't have enough money to do anything fancy, and we had to get back and start fishing. To this day Dawn and I go fishing or camping every year on our anniversary. It's an experience that neither of us would trade for anything else. Life is good.

CHAPTER 6

# Smooth sailing ahead

As our second fishing season began, things could not have been better. My good friend Kearlee had told me that if I treated the people right, they would come back. Man did they ever. Almost everyone we took fishing the first year came back. This time they came with their friends, and their friends came with others. My business almost tripled.

I was beginning to meet some very high powered influential people. The one thing that everyone had in common at the end of a day of fishing was that not only did they enjoy catching fish; they really enjoyed fishing without any crowds. As the Kenai River was already becoming a circus show, there were several days that I was the only boat on the Kasilof River. It was beautiful. It was what you would think Alaska was supposed to be.

I could not have been happier. I was making my living on this beautiful river which was still very much uncrowded. There was trouble on the horizon however as landowners on the river were starting to open their land for access to drift boats, which would surely bring more guides. I had no idea how much I was going to be part of the changes on the river and how many more guides were going to be showing up.

In the winter of 87-88, we decided to go back to Hawaii to spend the Christmas holiday. This time we would travel to three different islands. We were still traveling on a tight budget as we still didn't have much money but unlike our last trip to Hawaii this time we had friends there that I had taken fishing the summer before.

One such friend was Russell Yamashita who was an attorney from Honolulu. Russell knew that the big city wasn't for us. He set us up at a YMCA camp called Camp Erdman on the north shore of Oahu. Since it was the Christmas holiday, the camp was empty. We had a cabin with our own private beach all to ourselves for a cost of sixteen dollars a day while people in Waikiki were paying well over a hundred dollars a day sharing a beach with thousands of other people. Once again, there's the power of fishing and friends.

We had friends from Anchorage who had a house in Kona on the Big Island where we would spend a week. I spent every morning out reef fishing having no trouble catching fish. I would also watch a neighbor there leave with his boat and return at the end of the day with his catch of fish. I told myself I need to get to know this guy.

I walked over to his place one day while he was unloading fish to introduce myself. His name is Carl Taniyama. I told him I was from Alaska and gave him some smoked salmon. He in return gave me one of his fish he had caught that day. The fish was called a Paka Paka, which is the Hawaiian name for red snapper. It was one of the finest eating fish I have ever had. I knew that if I were ever to come back to this place, I was going to get to know this man better.

Before we returned to Alaska, I met a man through another friend of mine whose name was Bobby Dang. Bobby just so happened to own one of the oldest tour agencies in Hawaii. He had heard of me and my fishing business and was very interested in making a trip to Alaska to fish. This would be the beginning of the Hawaiian connection.

When we returned home, we had some very interesting news. Because Dawn had full class load for her college degree, she ended up with a failing grade in one of her classes, and the state was withholding her student loan check because of it. We were really counting on that check since we just spent what little money we had in Hawaii. From then until fishing season I got a job driving a taxi, filleting Cod for a cannery and delivered the local newspaper. All three jobs sucked but a man must do what a man must do.

It was times like this that helped me choose my political believes. I feel that people that want to live on welfare and claim they can't get a job are nothing more than a bunch of blood sucking parasites that have no class or pride and want to live of the people that do. I guess that you can tell by now that I'm not a bleeding-heart liberal.

As the 88-fishing season began, it was just like the year before. More and more people bringing their friends to the point I couldn't do it all. I would need to get someone else to fish for me. I was getting all these people that wanted to fish with me by my third year in business without spending a penny on advertising. My clients were doing it all for me. I also knew then that I must have been good at what I was doing to have all this business.

I asked a longtime fishing buddy of mine if he wanted to guide that summer. He took the summer off from his job and was more than happy to do so. I would soon learn a few lessons from doing this. As the summer went on all was going well. I had two boats fishing almost every day. Almost thirty percent of my business was from Hawaii. I was meeting more and more people who were going to become a huge part of my life.

That summer I took a man fishing whose name was Jonathan Blattmachr. Jonathan was and still is a very well-known tax attorney from New York City whose nephew would eventually become my first and only deckhand. He must have had a good time because he came back that fall with another friend of his George Goerig who was a tax attorney from Anchorage. George also owned a place on the Kenai River in Sterling.

We hit it off good from the time we met. The fishing that day was good as usual. At the end of the day, George mentioned to me that if we ever wanted to move out of Soldotna that he owned another place next to his in Sterling that he would rent to us. This was an offer that Dawn and I would think about very seriously.

By the end of summer, we could only call it another success story. We had all the business we could ever want while at the same time making more and more friends. Man, was my life ever changing!

CHAPTER 7

# MAKING CHANGES

The winter of 88-89 would prove to be very interesting, to say the least. Dawn was in her last year in school. She and I each took a course to get our private pilot's license. We figured if we were to sell our house, we could go buy an airplane.

During this time, we both decided to quit smoking cigarettes. At the time we were spending about a thousand dollars a year, which was enough to buy two round-trip airline tickets anywhere in the country. We figured if we quit we could go on a trip every year which is just what we did for many years. We called it our cigarette vacation. It was just another simple step to enhance the quality of our lives.

When Christmas time came around, we once again went back to Hawaii for a two-week vacation. I guess you could figure by now that we really enjoyed Hawaii. On the big island, we stayed at our friend's house where we stayed the year before. One of the first things I did was walk down the hill to see my new

Carl and Mitzi Taniyama

friend Carl Taniyama and his wife Mitzi who is one of the sweetest ladies I have ever met.

Carl and Mitzi are your typical Hawaiian people. They enjoy good food, good company, and cold beer. There my kind of people. Over time we became good friends. I had the privilege of introducing them to Alaska and my friends and family. They became very close friends with my mom and Max. Isn't it funny how friendships blossom like that?

Our friends were selling the house where we were staying at as well as everything else they had. One of the things they were selling that got the attention of Dawn and I, was a boat and an old dodge truck to pull it with. The boat was a twenty-four-foot Sea ray fully loaded and ready to fish, all for twelve thousand dollars. Now isn't this just interesting.

When we returned to Alaska, we had some serious decisions to make. It took about a month to decide we would sell the house in Soldotna, move to Sterling and rent the place from our new friend George and buy the boat in Hawaii. We didn't have enough money for the boat, so we borrowed what we needed from a friend which we would pay back when the fishing season started.

In February I flew back to Hawaii to buy the boat with the intentions of spending a few weeks fishing and learning the Hawaiian waters. The day I left the temperature was thirty below and had been that way for a week with no sign of it warming up anytime soon.

Since we just spent all the money we had and then some on this boat, Dawn took on a side job cleaning rooms along with going to school, and Brian got a job delivering newspapers. Dawn would get up early in the morning, take Brian on his paper route, drop him off at school and then go to school herself. When that was done, she would go clean rooms at the end of the day. What a woman. I don't know many women that would send their husbands off to Hawaii to fish in their new boat and do the kind of crap she did.

The first week I was there I caught no fish. I needed to learn to fish with live bait as the charter fleet was doing well using this method. Not having enough money for a charter, I would have to learn this on my own. I called home and told Dawn that I needed another week. She told me everything was fine, and that the temperature was now forty below. It was awfully hard to tell her how much fun I had fishing in eighty-degree weather.

The next week I found out my friends George and Jonathan were in Kona on business. They had a charter booked for two days and invited me along. Now was my chance to learn how to live bait. I told them not to tell the captain that I was a fishing guide in Alaska or that I had a boat in Kona. Somehow the captain found out so for two days we trolled with lures while the rest of the charter fleet fished with live bait. Needless to say, we didn't catch any Marlin. I eventually became friends with this captain, who was an old sea dog with a great reputation as a Marlin fisherman. He looked at me one day and said, "loose lips sink ships." How true it is.

Fishing in Hawaii

By the end of the second week I had still not caught any Marlin, but I was getting much closer. I called home and again told Dawn that I needed another week. She again told me that everything was fine, and the temperature was still forty below. I almost felt bad, but I was having way too much fun.

I soon met a local kid who taught me a few things about live baiting. It didn't take long to catch our first fish, a two hundred and forty-five-pound Blue Marlin. It was awesome. What was better yet is that when we came back into the harbor, the fish buyers come to you, you didn't go look for them. They were paying a dollar a pound for Marlin. Now not only am I catching fish, but I'm also making money doing it. This was great. All I had to do is go fish all day in the hot sun drinking cold beer and make money. This was way too easy. A few days later we caught a 286 pound marlin. Now life is good.

Me and my friend Jim Frary.
Life is good when your catching fish like this.

I was up at the boat wash area cleaning my boat after a day of fishing when a man came up and offered me sixteen thousand dollars for the boat which I just bought for twelve thousand. If he had come up to me a week earlier, I might have sold it, but I was so excited about catching fish that I turned it down. I called home and told Dawn that I was finally catching fish. She told me that the temperature was now fifty below and that it was time for me to get my ass back home.

After a few more days of fishing, I parked the boat at a friend's house for the summer and headed back to Alaska. When I got home, the temperature was twenty above. The cold snap was over. It was one of the worse cold snaps on record for the Kenai Peninsula, and I was in Hawaii fishing. I told Dawn that next winter we will go to Hawaii for six months and that I can make enough money with the boat that it won't cost us anything. It will be a six-month free vacation. It sure sounded good at the time.

That spring we sold our house and moved to Sterling where we would spend the next eighteen years. This would prove to be a good move as Soldotna was becoming a small city which Dawn and I didn't like and we would now live next to the Kenai River with a boat launch in our front yard.

When the fishing season began, it was business as usual. We had more and more people wanting to fish with us. My fishing buddy took the summer off from his job and guided for us again. I would soon learn that my friend was a much better fisherman than he was a guide which I find true in many fishing guides.

In late July at the end of King Salmon season, he came in from a fishing trip very upset with his clients because they didn't catch their limit of fish and walked off the job. Not knowing when or if he was even going to come back I would have to get someone else to fish for me as I already had two boats booked for the fall season. Dawn decided she would run a boat until I could find someone else. She was adventurous, willing to learn and already had plenty of experience running a drift boat. Dawn became the first women guide on the Kasilof River. She did great, and everyone enjoyed fishing with her.

One of my favorite things about fishing is trash talking. I love friendly competition. I love to talk it up to the point that all anyone wants to do is beat me. Let me tell you when we would come in at the end of a day of fishing and Dawn would have more fish than me or if she caught her limit first, man did I hear about it. It is what you call all in the name of fun.

I would have another friend of mine start guiding for me that fall. Now I would have three boats fishing. The greed factor was setting in. I had enough business to keep three boats fishing every day and many times making two trips a day. I had no idea what a big mistake I was making by doing this. All I knew is that I was becoming a big-time fishing guide with the attitude of the more clients, the better. How dumb I was.

When the fishing season was finally over, I again could not have been happier. Not only was my business still growing with no end in sight, but Dawn was now one of the guides which meant more money for us. If there was any bad news at all, it was that this would be the last year that we would have the Kasilof River mostly to ourselves. Things were going to change. We were also excited about the fact that Dawn was now finished with school and we were going to be spending the entire winter in Hawaii. Life is good or, so we thought.

CHAPTER 8

# Hawaii bound

When October came around, we were ready for what we thought was going to be a six-month free vacation. To make things easier for us our friend George, who is now our landlord told us that if we pay the utilities for the winter, he won't charge us any rent. He would also take care of our golden retriever for the winter. What a friend.

As soon as we arrived in Hawaii, the work began. We would have to find a place to rent and get Brian enrolled in school. We would also have to find a freezer locker to rent as we had twelve boxes of Salmon and other Alaska goodies. The one thing I learned about Hawaii is that if you have Salmon to barter with your much better off.

It took almost a month to find a place to rent. Until then we were staying in a one-room condo that was costing us four hundred a week. When we finally found the first and only house that was available to rent we took it. The rent for this small two-bedroom house was fourteen hundred a month plus electricity. We had to lease it for six months and pay a one-month deposit. We had only been in Hawaii for one month, and we were already running low on money.

The house was great. It was up at the fifteen hundred foot elevation above Kona with a great view of the ocean. At that level, it was like having free air conditioning. We could sit out on our lanai in the evenings and watch the sunset over the ocean while we drank our Pina Coladas. We had papaya and banana trees in our yard, so the fresh fruit was no problem. Now life is good.

I went to our friend's house to get the boat and bring it back to our place to get it ready to fish. I was in for another surprise. Because my boat was parked all summer without being run, the engine had plenty of corrosion. It would cost almost a couple thousand dollars to repair it before I would ever see the water. I had not planned on any of this. I was starting to wonder how much more this free vacation is going to cost.

I had Dawn and Brian come with me for the maiden voyage. We could not have been more excited. We were finally taking our boat out fishing and hopefully catch some fish and make some money. There was about a ten foot swell that day but no wind.

We were trolling about ten miles out from Kona when suddenly, the engine began to spit and sputter and then it quit. Talk about being scared shitless. The radio didn't work, and we were so excited to go fishing that we didn't even tell anyone that we were going. I could only see us floating away in the Pacific Ocean with no drinking water never to be seen again.

While I was looking the engine over, I discovered that the points were closed. The distributor bearing had corroded. While I was adjusting the points, Dawn starts puking over the side of the boat. Now I'm breathing the fumes from the engine and listening to her puke. It only took a moment before I was hanging over the other side puking. Brian was up in the front of the boat laughing his ass off watching us hanging over the boat.

By the time I got the engine started, the fishing was over. We headed straight back to Kona. Every five minutes or so the engine would quit, and we would go through the same procedure, adjust the points and puke. I had never been so glad to get back to land. What a way to start our Hawaiian fishing adventure.

For the next several trips out, I was skunked. I couldn't buy a fish out of that ocean. And it wasn't just me. The whole charter fleet was doing poorly. I learned that in Hawaii the fishing is usually slow in the winter and the winter before was unusually good. What a time to learn this. Not only was

I not catching any fish the boat was becoming a floating money trap. Every time I looked at the boat, it would cost me money for something.

The day before Thanksgiving I went on a turkey hunt with one of my Hawaiian friends and shot my first turkey. Not only did we each get a turkey, but we also shot a sheep and some pheasants. This free food was a blessing. Many people don't realize that the hunting in Hawaii is good enough that you can about live off the land. I was learning this the hard way.

Dawn took on a job at a small office product store working for five dollars an hour while I continued to figure out how to catch anything in the water. I started night fishing for a Hawaiian staple fish called an Opelo. On a good night I could make a hundred dollars, but most of the time it was much less. On some nights when the swell was up, I would have to fish all night puking my guts out waiting for daylight to come back in. I was beginning to think that this Hawaiian fishing sucks.

When Christmas time came around, we were so broke that we couldn't even afford a tree. The day before Christmas the trees were reduced from fifty to ten dollars, so we bought one. This was becoming a good test for Dawn, Brian and me to find out what kind of hardships we could live under.

I decided to give up on the idea that I could make any money fishing and decided to get a job. I started working for a moving company that paid seven dollars an hour. This wasn't much money, but it was better than what I was doing. It took both mine and Dawns paychecks just to pay the rent. We had very little money for food.

I went on a hunting trip and shot a Spanish goat and a pig. At our house, the dinner was either goat meat and rice or pig meat and rice. When we got sick of that, we would eat salmon. The one thing we weren't going to do was go to the welfare office and ask for food stamps. Screw that! We got ourselves into this mess, and we would get ourselves out of it.

Throughout that winter we had several friends and family travel from Alaska to visit us. We would take everyone fishing who wanted to go. We would never catch any fish, but we would have a good time. My parents came over in February, which would be there first time to Hawaii. I took Max on a three-day pig and sheep hunt up in the mountains. This would be my first-time hunting on public land. We shot a couple of pigs and no sheep. On the way down the mountain at the end of the hunt, we ran into a fish and game roadblock. The game warden asked how the hunting was. I told the man that the hunting was good and that we had a couple of pigs. The game warden then says, "that's the first violation boys, step out of the truck." Apparently, there's a season on pigs. This was news to me since all my hunting was done on private land where you didn't worry about that kind of stuff.

When it was all said and done with we each had multiple tickets and half our stuff was confiscated. When we drove up to the house, my mother came out all excited after not seeing us for three days and asked, "where's the pigs." I just looked at Max and said, "you tell her." Chalk it up to another one of lives interesting experiences.

Soon after my parents left, we decided to sell the boat. We really needed the money and we damn sure weren't coming back for another winter of this. Unfortunately, the fishing is so poor that very few people are looking for boats. Now I can't sell the boat that just a year before I could have easily sold for a profit.

In late April I headed home to get ready for fishing season. Dawn and Brian would stay there until Brian was finished with school. Dawn called me soon after I returned home and told me she

Dawns first marlin

found a buyer for the boat. We would sell it for nine thousand dollars. I have never been so happy to sell a boat and take a loss. She also told me that she went out fishing with a freind of ours and caught a 247 pound marlin, her first one. I was happy for her.

Our six-month free vacation didn't quite go as planned, but we had no regrets. At least we did it. The people we met and the experiences we had were worth more than money could ever buy. Twenty-eight years later we're still talking and laughing about it.

When we were telling people that we were going to Hawaii for the winter, I heard more people say that they had always wanted to do that. I have one suggestion to anyone who is thinking about doing something like this. Just do it. You only live once. All you can do is loose. That's easy.

Probably the single biggest thing we learned is that we love Alaska more than we thought we did. Never again did we ever leave Alaska for more than a week or two. One of the fondest memories I have of fishing after returning home wasn't catching a Salmon or Halibut. It was going out on a lake ice fishing for the day in the wilderness without seeing or hearing another human. Only in Alaska!

CHAPTER 9

# Still growing the business and Dawn starts one

When the 1990 fishing season began, I could not have been happier. I was already booked for the season before I even left Hawaii and after our Hawaiian adventure, making some money would be a treat.

What would make this season different is that I kept at least two boats fishing throughout the summer and four boats fishing for the fall Silver season. Not only was I keeping four boats fishing many times making two trips a day, I still couldn't take all the people fishing that wanted to hire me. I had all this business in just four or five years.

It was during this summer that I would take George's brother Ace fishing. Ace was a very successful dentist that enjoyed giving people advice on how to make money. When I was telling him about all these people that wanted to fish with me, he suggested I raise my prices. This would surely turn people away.

I remember driving to the Kasilof River one morning to meet four different groups of people that I had set up for fishing. On the way there I was thinking to myself, will all the guides be there on time? Will all the clients be happy with whom there fishing with? Will there be plenty of fish for everyone to catch? All this crap was going through my head. When I arrived at the river, there were people standing all over the place in small groups. I only knew one person from each group. As I was introducing myself to everyone and introducing them to their designated guides, I was starting to realize that I don't need all this crap.

I was accommodating all these people mostly for my own ego. For the small amount of money that I was making off the other boats, it was hardly worth my time and I was starting to get burned out from dealing with so many people. Things were soon going to change.

When the fishing season was over, we made an offer to our friend George to buy our place in Sterling. We would now become homeowners again. This would work out good as in seven years we would have it paid off.

When winter came, a job opening came up for a service technician at a local office supply store. This would work great for Dawn as it was a good paying job and how she qualified for it is kind of funny. When we spent the winter in Hawaii Dawn had got that job at the office supply store as a salesperson. There was an old copier there that kept breaking down, and on her free time she would work on it and get it going. By the time we left Hawaii, she knew plenty about copiers. Not only did she have a degree in computer electronics, she had all this experience on copiers because of a five dollar an hour job from our six months not so free fishing vacation. Isn't it funny how that works?

In January, Dawn and I along with another couple of friends went on a one-week fishing trip to Cabo San Lucas, Mexico. The Marlin fishing was outstanding. In two days of fishing, we hooked twenty and landed twelve. Fishing like this was unheard of in Hawaii.

When we weren't Marlin fishing, we would spend our time fishing in front of our resort and drinking cold beer. I was giving all my fish to the Mexicans who would follow me up and down the beach practically begging me for them. Giving these people my fish helped me realize how well I have it and how much I love America.

When we returned home, the Persion Gulf war was just starting. All the oil companies were increasing security for the threat of terrorism. I took on a job as a security guard at the Swanson River oil field. All I did was drive around the oil field viewing wildlife, and I learned how to play Nintendo.

When the war was over my job was over. This would be the last time I would work for anyone else for the next twenty years.

In the latter part of winter, I told Dawn that I was going to clear enough of our property to make a lawn and build a cabin to put our guests in. She looked at me as if I was going crazy. I took an ax, and within two days I had it cleared.

When spring arrived, the race was on to build the cabin as I already had it booked for July. I had plenty of help from my friends since I had very little knowledge about building anything and I was running out of time with fishing season arriving. This cabin idea was going to prove to be a very good decision.

John O'Hurley, or to you Seinfield fans, Mr. Peterman

The 91-fishing season was going to be much different than any other. I decided I was only going to fish with people who I wanted to fish with and I was going to raise my prices. I was no longer going to have other guides fish for me. This was only my fifth year in business, and I was already weeding people out. I loved it.

I also decided to get licensed for the Kenai River. The Kasilof River was beginning to get crowded, and I figured if I had to fish in a crowd, I might as well fish the Kenai where I could start my trips from my front yard. The middle Kenai was still not very crowded with power boats, and it made for a nice fifteen-mile drift from my house to Soldotna. The fishing in the Kenai wasn't as good as the Kasilof, but at least the Kings were much larger.

When the season was over it was another success. I was now fishing seven days a week since I was the only boat and making more money for it. What amazed me the most is that I still couldn't take all the people fishing that wanted to fish with me. I also decided to build another cabin.

That summer I had the privilege to meet and become good friends with the first salt water fishing guide in Ninlchik. His name was Bob Chenier.

When Bob talked about fishing the best thing you could do is shut up and listen. The man was the best and he taught me allot about saltwater King fishing which was great at that time. I want to share a story about Bob which to this day I think is the best fishing story I have ever heard.

When Bob retired from fishing he would walk the beach all the time with his wife Ida. While walking the beach one day he sees three old people he knows in a small boat coming in to the beach towing a giant Halibut behind the boat. Bob helped them load the boat and the giant fish and took it up to get it weighed. There was no scale in Ninilchik large enough to weigh the fish so they would have to take it to Homer to get it weighed.

Bob Cheiner with what could of been the new world record Halibut.

The old lady who had caught the fish told Bob screw it, just slap a weight on it, take a picture and fillet it which is what they did. When it was all said and done with the estimated weight of the fish was 466lbs, it was 94 ¾ inches long and was 29 years old which would have been the new world record. All this from three old people fishing in a little boat in thirty feet of water. What a great fishing story. Bob died of a heart attack while walking the beach with his wife Ida on September 4th, 2008. He was 86. I consider myself privileged to of ever had such a friend.

That fall I also had the pleasure to take Barbara O'Mally fishing on the upper Kenai. The O'Mally family are very well known in Anchorage and O'Mally road is named after her father. Barb was a nurse in Anchorage who was also hooked on fishing. Within no time at all it seemed like I was taking what seemed like half the doctors and nurses in Anchorage fishing. Barbara also introduced me to Dennis Maloney who was a very well known attorney from Anchorage. Dennis and I became good friends and remained that way until he died a few years ago.

Bob and myself catching kings in Cook Inlet     Barbara O'Mally with a nice king

Dennis Maloney with his daughter Bridget

Dennis with his friend Stan Fenner. The king Stan is holding was 81 lbs.

In the winter of 92, I went to school in Seward to get my Coast Guard captains licenses. That spring I bought my first saltwater boat and started Halibut fishing. Now I could do Halibut trips myself instead of passing them on to someone else. This was going to work out well for me as well as my clients.

Now I was fishing the Kenai River, the Kasilof River and the ocean. I could take a group on a three or four-day fishing trip and do something different each day. If the fishing was poor in one place, I would just simply fish somewhere else. My clients could not have been more pleased. They were getting to do a large variety of fishing all with the same guide, and I didn't have to do the same stuff each day.

For the next few years, it was business as usual. I was fishing as much as I wanted to, which was pretty much every day all summer and making good money. I was starting to get much more selective about who I would take fishing. I felt that life could not be much better.

In 93, while Dawn was working as a service technician for The Office Place, she often heard people ask if they recharged toner cartridges. The answer was no. No one on the Kenai Peninsula did. These were common phone calls.

Dawn did a little research and discovered it was a big business in the lower forty-eight. She found a company in Seattle that sold kits for recharging toner cartridges for the cost of eight hundred dollars. That winter we went to Seattle for a Seahawks football game, and Dawn bought the kit. She said she wanted to quit her job and give it a try. All I asked is that she waits until the fishing season to quit.

As spring approached Dawn gave the office store a six-week notice that she's leaving and tells them of her intentions. Her boss told her that her idea wouldn't work as there weren't enough people on the Kenai Peninsula to support it. Dawn wasn't discouraged.

As the six weeks were coming to an end, the office store had received a few phone calls from there costumers asking why she was leaving as they liked her and the quality of her work. Dawn's boss called her into her office and offered her a two dollar an hour raise to stay. Dawn was already making thirteen bucks an hour with health benefits, which was a really good job for the Kenai area at that time. Dawn turned it down. She had made up her mind; she was going to have her own business, win or lose.

Dawn's new business would be called Toner Resource. It only took a few weeks for word to get out about it and so it began. Toner Resource took off like a rocket. Dawn made more money in her first year in business than she did working for the office store. Dawn couldn't have been happier. Not only was she making money with her new business, but she was also saving people money. It was such a no-brainer. All this from an eight-hundred-dollar kit and a little courage!

In the fall of 94, I went fishing at a lodge in Katmai National park with my good freind Dennis Maloney. This lodge offers outstanding fishing and accommodations all for about a thousand dollars a day per person. Dennis was the attorney for the lodge and would take me along as his guest.

This would be the first time I would see people pay this kind of money to fish. Not only were they paying that kind of money to fish, but it was also all catch and release fishing. For the person who could afford it, it was money well spent. Everything about this lodge was excellent. I was soon going to learn about the kind of people that pay that kind of money.

I decided to change my business around a little by offering full accommodations for allot more money. All people had to do is arrive in Anchorage, and I would take care of the rest. This sounded like an easy way to make money. The first group met my expectations. They were four old men that wanted everything taken care of for them. I made more money in three days than I made my first year in business. This was way too easy.

I figured I would only have to fish a few days a week and make more money than I was. There was only one problem. These people were here for more than just fishing. They were here do be wined and dined. I was becoming a servant more than a fishing guide. The money was good, but I didn't like it. I'm a fisherman after all.

This great idea I had only lasted a few years before I said screw it. I was going to go back to only taking people fishing who I enjoyed fishing with. I wasn't going to make as much money, but at least I could enjoy myself.

CHAPTER 10

# Avalanche

On January 12th, 1997, I snow machined up into the Kenai mountains for a week to gather moose and caribou antlers and do some grouse hunting. Gathering antlers is not only fun, but it can also be quite profitable as a person can make several hundred dollars in a day.

A few days later I was high up on a mountain ridge picking up caribou antlers. I figured since this was one of the few areas that had cell service, I would call a friend of mine Lance Domonoske and tell him that the picking was good and rub it in a little. One of my favorite things to do is have fun with something good.

Lance was also a drift boat fishing guide who served on the Kenai-Soldotna fish and game advisory committee and was one of the finest antler hunters I have ever met. He was also a master carver of antlers, and his work could be found all across the United States. After hearing that I was up in the mountains picking antlers the next day there was Lance. I had a feeling he would show up. We spent the day running all over the mountains looking for antlers.

That night we stayed at an old trapper's cabin that I had stayed at many times before. We talked about what life must have been like back when the trapper built the cabin in 1920. We talked about our own lives, our wife's, kids and just how good we had it. We also talked about our own mortality. We both agreed that we would rather die doing something like what we were doing than to lay in a hospital bed with cancer or some other kind of crap.

Later the next day on the 17th, we decided to make our way out of the mountains and head home. We stopped at a lookout point to get one last look at the high country. Sure enough, Lance spots a moose over a mile away on another mountain. Not only does he see the moose he thinks he sees an antler lying next to it. Hell, I could hardly see the moose let alone the antler. I guess that's what made him the best.

He looked at me and said he must go see if it's an antler. He would have to snow machine across a valley, which was resurrection pass, just to get halfway there, then snowshoe the rest of the way across the face of a mountain. He figured it would take him about two to three hours. We decided to meet at the bottom of the mountain at three o'clock.

When Lance took off across the valley, I thought about going with him, but I didn't as I was tired and wanted to get home, so I headed down the mountain with all our gear to wait. While waiting for Lance, I could hear three different Bull Moose fights going on around me. You could hear horn to horn combat echoing through the valley. When three o'clock came around Lance didn't show. Then it was five o'clock and still no Lance, and now it's dark with a full moon. This was not part of the plan. We were supposed to be home by now.

I unhooked the sled from my machine and headed back up the mountain. I followed his tracks across the valley to the other mountain where I found his snowmachine parked. At this point I figured he must have found the mother lode of antlers to be this late.

The moon was so bright that night that I didn't even need a flashlight to follow his footprints. In less than one hundred yards I walked into an avalanche. My heart sank to my feet. I couldn't believe it. I yelled out his name with no response. There was no cell service where I was at, so the phone was no good. All I could do was turn my back and walk away. That part hurt. There was a chance he could be on the other side of the avalanche, so I put a sleeping bag on his machine just in case.

It was a seventeen-mile ride out of the mountains to where my truck was parked. All I could think about was what am I going to tell everyone. How would I tell his lovely wife Laurie or his young kids? All this crap was going through my mind. I felt terrible.

When I got home, I called the State Troopers. They immediately began organizing a search and rescue. The next phone call I got was from Laurie. In her own cute little voice, she asks me "where's my husband"? Let's just say it was a very difficult phone conversation. When she started breaking down all I could do was tell her to get to my house as soon as possible.

Word was out that Lance was in trouble. By midnight there were several hundred-people volunteering for the search party. It was an impressive sight to see. That tells you what kind of person Lance was and what kind of people Alaskans are. The people of Sterling really came through that night.

The National Guard tried to get a helicopter down from Anchorage but had to turn back due to a snow storm. By the next morning, they were able to reach the avalanche site with a rescue team. After flying over the avalanche site, they were able to see that Lance never made it to the other side. Now the rescue was going to turn into a body recovery.

With the help of a trained Border collie named Zip, Lance's body was recovered in just a few hours. There were four of us that carried his body into the National Guard helicopter for the ride to Kenai, and I wish I could remember who the other three were but I do remember them as being very close friends with Lance. As we all walked away I couldn't help but think that just a day before Lance and I were talking about how we would prefer to die. Lance died doing what he loved to do which is just the way he wanted to go.

Tim Rowlett and Alan Holt were two very close freinds of Lance. They put this cross up there on the mountain which I believe is still there today.

Alaska can be an unforgiving place. There are more people that die from accidental death in Alaska per capita than any other state in the nation. When you're surrounded by nature, bad things can happen. This is what makes Alaska so special. I would much rather take my chances on a mountainside in Alaska than a traffic jam in California.

Lances' memorial service had to be held at the local school gymnasium as it was the only place large enough to hold all the people and it was packed. Laurie's family all came up from California to be there. A few days after this I took her dad on a snow machine trip to do some ice fishing and to get to know each other. We had a bottle of whisky to drink and that's just what we did. Man did we get drunk. I think he needed it as much as I did. I can't remember if we caught any fish or not but we did have a good time. I think that was the last time I ever drove drunk.

This is a strange story, but I have to say it. A week or two after this I took Lances oldest son Levi, up to the mountains to show him where his dad died and showed him why his dad loved it so much up there. When we got up there, the mountain pass was socked in with fog. Thick fog like you would see in the ocean, not the mountains. I had never even seen fog in the mountains where this was.

The only way we were able to get to the avalanche sight was because of all the tracks from the search and rescue. As we approached the avalanche site, the fog started to leave the valley and uncovered the avalanche and stopped not far past the bottom of it. At first, I didn't think anything of it. I pointed out to Levi where they dug his dads body out and told him I would leave him alone and would wait for him on the other side of the hill. After about ten or fifteen minutes Levi came around the hill and said he was ready to go. As we rode across resurrection pass to leave, I looked back one last time. The fog bank moved over and covered the avalanche back up. Now I'm not a religious man, but I got a funny hunch there was more to that than just a coincidence. I will never forget it.

Lance was an avid Drift boater and did his part to promote it. He made it on the front page of the Anchorage Daily News on October 14th 1996 with an article called throttle down or power up. He was very well respected with all the drift boat guides, me included. When Laurie sold

Lances drift boat another guide bought it. It was a bright blue boat and the only one like it. When that guide made its first trip down the river I heard all the guides stopped doing what they were doing to show respect to the boat and Lance. I wish I was there that day. He was a good man.

Laurie and the kids became family that night and remain so. She was remarried a few years later to a good guy who adopted her two kids, Logan and Lindsey, to add to his own two kids, Kyle and Ashley, and they all still live here. Lindsey got married a few years ago to a good man and they just had there first child, a beautiful little girl. Logan is getting married this coming summer to a really cool girl. God do I ever love life. To take something so tragic and it ends up with such a cool ending. Life goes on.

There is one final thing about this story that I want to share. Exactly one year to the day after Lance was killed I was riding my snow machine up the Swanson river to do some ice fishing at one of my favorite lakes. As I was riding I looked off to one side and there was a large moose antler sitting on top of the snow so easy to be seen that a blind man could have spotted it. It was almost as if it were set there for me to find. Every time I look at it I smile and think of Lance.

CHAPTER 11

# Building our first house

When the 97-fishing season started, it was going to be just another season. It was no longer as exciting as it was a few years back. The Kasilof River was getting much more crowded with guides, and the middle Kenai River was getting full of power boats, and the fishing wasn't as good as in the past. Everything was changing and after the winter before with the avalanche and all; I really wasn't even looking forward to it.

When fall arrived, I couldn't have been happier. Not only was fishing season over, but we also made our last land payment to our friend George. For seven years we made five-hundred-dollar monthly land payments, and now it was finally ours. We were no longer in debt to anyone.

We had always talked about building a house when we paid off our place, and now it was time. No more living in a trailer house. Dawn's dad came up from Minnesota in late September and would spend one month helping us move the trailer and working on the foundation for the new house. He would be a big help as I was still fishing often.

On October 1st we sold our trailer and had it removed. Dawn and I moved into one of our cabins in our backyard and Dawns dad stayed at our neighbors. Everything we owned was under a tarp in our backyard. We were going to live with our two dogs, a phone line and a computer in our twelve by twenty cabin. This was going to be a long winter.

The next day, with no building plans and not much of an idea of what kind of a house I was even going to build, I had the heavy equipment come in and dig the hole for the foundation. The only thing I knew for sure was the size of the house I wanted to build. This was going to be a new experience for me, and I looked forward to the challenge.

For the next month, I spent every day pounding nails watching the house come together. There were many times I would have friends come by and give me a hand. I really found out who my friends were. It was quite humbling. I also had some friends tell me that I couldn't do this or do that and that I would need to hire a professional. My answer to that was bullshit. There's nothing I can't do and the only way to learn it was doing it yourself and it's also a lot more rewarding. Plus, I didn't have the money to hire anyone anyway.

When December came around our cabin was growing smaller and now our sewer line froze. For the rest of the winter, we would have no sewer which means no toilet. It was now honey bucket time. A five-gallon bucket worked just fine. This wasn't a problem for Dawn and me. How many women or men from the city would be willing to do this? I guess that's why Dawn and I make a good team.

When it came time to taping and mudding the sheetrock, I learned there were a few things I couldn't do, and taping was one of them. I called around to some of the sheetrock outfits to find out what it would cost. I knew then that I was in trouble. I didn't have that kind of money.

There was a guy who I barely knew had offered to help me with the sheetrock if I needed it when I first started the house. I called him and asked if the offer was still there. He came by and worked every day for ten days until it was done. Again, I was humbled. He didn't even want any money, but I gave him every penny I had. What a lifesaver. We became good friends after this. The power of friends is truly awesome.

On March 21st we moved into our new house. It wasn't complete yet, but it was good enough, and besides, we were out of money. We had spent every penny we had on it. It was also Dawns birthday. What a way to celebrate it.

In the six months since I had started the house, I took one week off to go deer hunting on Kodiak Island. Other than that, I worked every day on the house. I would spend the next two winters completing it. This would drive my good friend Dennis Maloney nuts. He offered me ten thousand dollars to finish it. I turned it down.

All I know is that it's a good feeling to have friends that are willing to loan you that kind of money and it's a better feeling to own my house debt free. This is another reason why I love Alaska. Where else can a person build a house with no plans, no permits, no inspectors or any of that other crap? All I had was an idea, a little bit of money and the courage to do it myself. All I can say is only in Alaska. Life is good.

CHAPTER 12

# The Kasilof fish camp

In the summer of 98, I was fishing on the upper Kasilof River and noticed some flagging tape along the river. I found this to be kind of strange as I thought all this land up there was the Kenai National Wildlife Refuge.

I came back a few days later and noticed two signs on the river that said Land for Sale University of Alaska. One sign at the upper end of the sale and one at the bottom end. I couldn't believe it. At first, I was sick to see it as I thought all this land was wilderness. I also thought that if this is the case, I'm getting in on it.

The next day I had the day off, so my friend George and I went back up to look the land over. There were ten lots to choose from. Out of the ten parcels, there were only two that didn't have any bluff or any swamp. George and I each got a partner and agreed to bid on these two pieces and not tell anyone else about it. Also, somehow the signs and flagging tape were removed. That's all I know.

About a month later George and I both get letters in the mail saying congratulations your bids were accepted. No one bid against us. I guess no one could find where the land was located. Again, that's all I know.

Now this land has world class fishing right in the front yard. It has a gravel bar for sockeye fishing. Fall Silver and Steelhead fishing right off the bank and brown bears in the fall dragging up all the old dead Kings that wash up. It's a dream piece of property.

For the first few years, we used it for a tent camp. It was kind of nice having my own place to be able to cook lunch for my clients and accommodate everything else. Each year we would have a one-hour sockeye derby on the fourth of July. Big fish take all the money. It was a blast. The derby got so big that one year our friends from Canada came up for it. They pitched their tent with us and helped celebrate America's independence. It was way cool.

One year a good client of mine, Super Dave brought Monsignor Jack Campbell, a priest friend with him to say a mass and to bless the property. While father Jack was setting up his military mass kit, he realized he forgot the wine. The priest tells Dave "I'm sorry, but I can't do the mass with no wine, but I can still bless the property." Dave looked at me and asked if I had any wine up here. I told him no that the only thing I have up here is some vermouth that I keep stashed in a fish tote for my gin martinis. Father Jack looks at us and says vermouth will work. Apparently, in the Catholic religion, it must have a certain amount of alcohol content to use in the mass. This was news to me. Either way, the mass did go on. And Father Jack blessed our property. It was a really cool sight to witness.

After a few years of tent camping, it was time to build our first cabin. It would be a sixteen by sixteen-foot cabin. I did the dirt work for it in the fall and spent the winter building it. Dawn and I snow machined in to insulate it, and we would sleep on the floor for the first night. I walked out on the frozen river and looked at our little cabin glowing in the dark. I was proud.

Hauling plywood ten sheets at a time

Dawn nailing the deck down

My partner on the property was my hunting partner from Kodiak, Gary who now wanted a cabin also. The following year over the 4th of July holiday we built cabin number two. We took one hour off for the derby and other than that we worked.

Then I built the wood-fired sauna. Then the shower house and a few sheds. I kind of got carried away. I eventually built a small house several years later that I will talk about later. Either way, it's an awesome piece of property to come and get away from it all. I love it as much now, twenty years later as I did when we got it. It was here that I spent the winter writing this book and feeding eagles. Life is good.

Getting ready to stand the first walls, with a North Carolina work crew. My brother Steven, cousin Kevin and friend Herbie. Notice the Kasilof River in the background.

CHAPTER 13

# Fish Politics and Burning Out

For the next four years, the fishing business was as good as it gets but was also becoming less fun. I was completely done fishing the Kenai River. The Kasilof River was getting more and more crowded, but the fishing was still good, and now power boats were starting to show up. I could just see it becoming another Kenai River.

When I first started guiding the Kenai River, there weren't many guides fishing the middle river. There were probably as many drift boats fishing as power boats. This wouldn't last long.

The last day I ever guided the Kenai it was a bloodbath. It was opening day to bait on the middle river, and every guide from the lower river was there. There was power boat guides packed in every hole. They would hook a King, go down the river, land it and power back up and do it again. And they wonder what happened to the great King fishing that the Kenai was famous for.

For the last four years that I guided, I served on the Kenai-Soldotna Fish and Game advisory board, which I was elected to after my friend Lance was killed in the avalanche. I had one goal in mind, getting power boats off the Kasilof River. I will never forget standing in front of the Alaska Board of Fish in Anchorage testifying on what was happening on the Kasilof River with all the Kenai River guides sitting behind me. The board agreed with me and decided to ban fishing from a motorized vessel on the Kasilof River.

I couldn't believe it. I was so happy driving out of Anchorage knowing this only to find out the next day that it would only last until July 31st, the end of King salmon season. I was told that at the last minute the Kenai River guides association requested it and the board passed it which really wouldn't surprise me. The issue with power boats was never in the spring but in the fall when the water was high.

The Kenai River guides association and the Kenai River sport fishing associations are two groups I am proud to say I had nothing to do with. Each year they host the Kenai River Classic, which is in my opinion, nothing more than a political fundraiser to get commercial fishing shut down or drastically reduced in Cook Inlet, so more Kings can make it in the river to be killed by sport fishermen.

Just a few years ago they had to move the Classic to the fall for Coho fishing because the King fishing sucked so bad. The last year they had it during King season I believe there were only three or four Kings caught for a few hundred people. It was a really small amount of fish for the amount of people. It couldn't have happened to a better bunch of people.

One year the owner of a tackle store in Soldotna called and asked if I would take Senator Stevens and another U.S. senator, fishing on the upper Kenai for a day of trout fishing. Both senators were here for the Classic. Now most people, especially a fishing guide would have jumped all over it considering that at the time Senator Stevens was the longest-serving Republican senator in U.S. history. He was a very powerful man that did a lot of good for Alaska. I proudly turned it down, and I'm a Republican.

He then tells me "no this is big time, this is Senator Stevens." I believe my words to him were I could really care less if it was the president of the United States I wasn't taking anyone fishing who was here for the Classic. That was the last time he ever called me, like it really hurt me. All I can say is the last six years I guided, I never fished the Kenai River, and I lived next to it with a boat launch in my front yard. I was too good for that.

I was spending more of my time on the salt water where I could at least get away from the crowds and keep my sanity. It costs more money to fish the saltwater with bait, fuel, deckhand, etc. and get the crap scared out of you in rough water from time to time but at least I could be alone and give my clients a quality trip.

I was getting tired of having to produce fish. People expect to catch fish when they're on a charter. I couldn't blame them. That's why they hired me. People would show up at my place with empty fish boxes with the hopes of filling them. And, this is what usually happened. Catching fish was easy. It just wasn't in my heart anymore.

This might sound kind of strange, but the day 9-11 happened, I just so happened not to be fishing. After watching TV in total disbelief of what had just happened, I said screw this and went and played a round of golf. Thank God I didn't shoot a hole in one. Sure couldn't celebrate it.

My retirement party. The lei I am wearing was sent to me from my friends Carl and Mitzi Taniyama. Notice the giant martini glass. Life is good.

The next day I took my friend Jonathan Blattmachr and his friends fishing. He was totally freaked out about what happened since he is from New York City. The catching fish meant nothing. When I returned home, my clients who were scheduled to fish with me the next day called me from Anchorage. I didn't know these people, which was rare as ninety-five percent of my business was repeat business. They tell me they could still come down and fish or I could cancel it if I wanted to. It was up to me. I told them to come on down. We're not letting crap like this stop us.

Those days of fishing and every trip after that for the rest of the season were some of the most enjoyable days of fishing that I had had in years. Not because we caught fish, that was easy but just the opposite. No one cared if we caught fish or not. We did lots of talking. Things about life in general, what would be and what could be kind of stuff. It was just what fishing was supposed to be.

It was also during this time that I decided that I wanted to go back to being a fisherman and not a fishing guide. I was going to retire from guiding. I announced in my Christmas letter that I sent to all my clients that 2002 was going to be my final year.

On September 15th, 2002, at the ripe age of forty-four I retired, debt free I might add. Man, what fishing and Alaska did for me. Not bad for a pot smoking high school dropout. Or better yet, double dropout. Life is just so damn good.

CHAPTER 14

# Saying goodbye

If anything was harder than starting the fishing business, it was getting out of it. All the people I took fishing over the years who were once just clients had become friends, good friends. I got to know their families, their kids, wife's, grandkids, pet dogs, you name it. Some people took it personally, while others understood. My heart was no longer in it. I did bootleg a few trips for some of my favorite people for the first few years after I retired, but that was it. The fact was these people were my friends and remain that way today.

The name of my business was Peninsula Adventures. People didn't come here to fish with Peninsula Adventures; they came to fish with me. That's one reason I never sold my business. I would have just screwed someone.

I want to share with you some really cool stories of some of my favorite guests and what they did for me and why it was so hard to quit.

### Super Dave

In my first year of guiding there was a bad plane crash in our local area that killed several people. Dave Snyder owned an insurance settlement company in California and was up here taking care of claims. He had heard of me and booked a day of fishing.

There began the California connection. Dave came up every year after that with a large group of people until the year I quit. California became my number one state where a bunch of my clients came from, all from that one day of fishing.

One-year Dave brought me a set of Callaway golf clubs and told me I needed to start playing golf. Those clubs might have been free, but that was it. For the next several years I spent a ton of money on that crazy game and had a lot of grief. Thanks a lot Dave!

In December of 2001, Dave invited Dawn and I down to California to play a little golf and to go watch the Rose Bowl, which was also going to be the national championship that year between Miami and Nebraska. All-expense paid. All we had to do was get there.

All I can say is that was the first Rose Bowl after 9-11, and when the national anthem ended, and the fighter jets flew over the stadium, there were eighty thousand people chanting USA, USA, USA. It probably lasted at least five minutes. I will never forget it.

I have never been prouder to be an American as I was at that moment. It was awesome. At half time they brought the pilots out on the field and it all started again. As I write this, I get a tear in my eye just thinking about it. It also makes me think of all the NFL players that want to kneel for the National Anthem. What a bunch of parasites. I have not watched another NFL game since then. I love football, but I love our flag and our country much more. What an insult to our military who have fought and sacrificed for our freedom.

In October 2002, Dave called me and asked what I'm up to. I tell him, I'm up at my cabin watching the river flow by. He then tells me "get your ass down the river and get to Anchorage. You're flying out at 1:00 am, I will pick you up in LA tomorrow, and we're going to game six of the World Series and if the Angels win were going to game seven".

That was probably the fastest I ever packed my stuff and oared down the river. When I got home, Dawn was just getting home from a Recharge toner convention in Las Vegas and had won a thousand bucks from a slot machine. She threw me some money and showed me a picture of her with Robin Williams who she got to meet in Vegas.

At the Anchorage airport, I see a lawyer and his wife who I didn't care for very much were on the same flight as I'm on. They were flying first class which means I'm going to have to walk past them on the plane. When I walked on the plane, he sees me and tells me they're going to Mazatlán with his chest all puffed up in his big seat and then asks me where I'm going. Let's just say I shot down his Mazatlán crap. I was the envy of the first class.

The next night at the World Series out of all crazy things I could not believe who was sitting two rows in front of me? Robin Williams. What a small world. He was getting pictures with people if you took off your Angels hat and put on his Giants hat. What a guy. We did end up going to game seven as game six was the greatest comeback in World Series history, and I was there thanks to my good friend Dave.

To make things even crazier, Dave calls me the next spring and asks if I would like to go to games one and two of the Stanley Cup, as the Anaheim Ducks were in it that year and Dave was a season ticket holder.

Super Dave

Now Dawn is a hockey nut. She even played in a womens league into her sixties. I told Dave that I would love to go, but I know someone else who would love to go even more. Let's just say Dawn went to games one and two of the Stanly Cup thanks to the generosity of a man I met through the simple act of fishing.

One last thing I would like to say about Dave was when my friend Lance was killed in the avalanche his wife Laurie was from California. She had no other immediate family here. They all lived in California, and we thought she was going to go back there. Dave was going to offer her a job down there if she needed it, just to be a good man. Dave and I remain very good friends today. Life is good.

Bobby the Hawaiian

## Bobby the Hawaiian

What can I say? The second time we went to Hawaii, a client of mine introduced me to Bobby Dang. Bobby was a very prominent man in the tourism industry and just so happened to love fishing. We immediately became friends. The following summer Bobby took his first trip to Alaska to fish with me and there it began. He came every year to fish up to the point that he loved it so much that he bought land on the Kasilof River and built his own fishing lodge.

Now Bobby was one of Hawaiian Airlines largest customers at the time. I believe he would buy about a million dollars' worth of tickets in advance to put together his own trips to Hawaii. The day Hawaiian airlines filed for chapter eleven to reorganize, Bobby was in Alaska fishing with me. I remember Bobby getting a phone call from the airline letting him know what they were doing before it even went public. It was then that I realized that this man was big time in Hawaii.

One winter Bobby paid my way to Hawaii to fish with him on the island of Molokai, where he also had a place. All I had to do was make my way to Anchorage. It was a great trip. Bobby paid for everything. I couldn't even buy my own beer, and Bobby's not a drinker. What a generous man.

The following winter Dawn, Brian and I went back to Hawaii for Christmas. Bobby met us at the Honolulu airport and gave us three roundtrip tickets to Molokai, the keys to his truck which he kept parked at the airport there and the keys to his place and told us to have fun. Once again, what generosity!

Several years later the Rolling Stones came to Hawaii to play at Aloha Stadium. Our attorney, Dennis Maloney, who was also a very good friend called me and said he had two extra tickets and asked me if Dawn and I wanted to go to the concert. I couldn't say yes fast enough.

These tickets came on short notice, so we only had a few days to make our arrangements. It wasn't long after that when Dennis calls me back and tells me that all the lodging is full in Honolulu. It just so happened that Bill Gates was in town and had paid for a private concert with the Rolling Stones for him and his guests who included President Bush Sr. and Margaret Thatcher from England. There was also a PGA golf tournament going on at that time. Honolulu was packed. So, I gave Bobby a call. Let's just say we got our rooms, and our transportation is taken care of to and from the concert and everything else we needed, all from a good friend that I had met through the simple act of fishing. To this day we remain very good friends.

I want to share one last thing about Bobby that he and I still laugh about today. He was here with a group of people one year in July King fishing with me when the Sockeyes hit the Kenai River in force.

I told him that if they wanted to take the day off from King fishing the next day that I would let them catch my winters supply of Sockeyes that night and they could catch themselves some to take back to Hawaii. I told them that I wanted fifty for myself. They were all for it.

When it got to its darkest time in the evening, Bobby and his buddy started in. They were catching fish faster than I could clean them. We were up to fifty-five fish when suddenly, I see two people approaching from upriver. Then the badges come out and the announcement "Alaska State Troopers"!

Just great, this is all we need. Bobby is still fishing not aware that there's a raid going on. I set my knives on the cleaning table and slowly turned away only to hear the words "sir, don't do it." I took off at a dead run, and one of the game wardens took chase after me. He could only chase me so far before he would have to go back to the other warden with all the activity.

I ran into my house, turned off my lights and told Dawn that there's a raid going on. I changed my clothes and went back down hiding in the trees just to watch Bobby and his buddy get tickets. All our fish and tackle were confiscated.

We met up an hour or so later and got a good laugh about it. No one could believe I could run so fast. In hip boots, I might add. It was pretty cool.

Bobby Dang (standing) having fun digging steamer clams in Kachemak Bay.

## The Fighter Pilots

I did not meet these guys until later in my career, and all I can say is wow, what a bunch. These guys were retired military pilots who came to Alaska for two things, fishing and drinking. Neither one of these took priority over the other. Our friendships were immediate.

They always came in late July when the Sockeyes were running in the Kenai. If we fished all day and caught nothing, it was no big deal. These boys were real fishermen. As a fisherman myself, one of my favorite things about fishing is pulling a good prank on someone, and these guys were no different. This is where the fun starts.

A good friend of mine was a good actor and played the part of being a game warden really well. I would take a few of these guys down to the river, set them up with snagging hooks and get them snagging Sockeyes, which I might say is very illegal.

I would give them a minute or two to fish and then bring in my game warden to bust them. It was awesome. One guy even tried to bribe his way out of it. Even better yet, once they got busted and found out it was just a joke; all they wanted to do is bust their other buddies. This is where the story really gets good.

I had two of them, Spanky and Doc, which was there call names, set up for snagging and I was filming it as if I were filming their Alaskan adventure. Spanky sees my game warden coming and takes off running back to his cabin and leaves Doc for dead meat. So much for the military fight together and die together crap. They sure weren't taking a ticket together.

Once we busted Doc all he wanted to do was to get revenge on Spanky. Doc went back to the cabin and told Spanky that the man is out there and wants to see him. When Spanky came out of the cabin, he had already changed his clothes and knew that this wasn't going to be good.

Now, my game warden friend is going to nail him for felony evading of a law officer on top of a snagging ticket. We had Spanky sweating bullets until he found out it was just a joke. Now the story even gets better.

Spanky's son-in-law Chris, is a Las Vegas motorcycle police officer. The following year Spanky brings him for his first fishing trip to Alaska. We get him set up on the river snagging. There were about six of them in the group, and everyone was in on the prank.

For this stunt, I brought in two game wardens. The bust was on. As everyone was pulling out their fishing licenses, I walked up and asked if there was a problem. My game warden asked if I knew these guys and then tells me to show him my license. I told him something like "go screw yourself asshole, I wasn't fishing". All this time the real cop is standing on the bank holding a fishing rod with a snagging hook on it, watching in total disbelief of what was happening. When he found out it was a joke he wasn't impressed. I still laugh every time I think about it.

The Fighter Pilots

One of these guys lived in Washington DC and worked at the pentagon sitting in with the Joint Chiefs of Staff. He always told Dawn and I if we ever came to DC he would give us a personal tour through the pentagon and Arlington national cemetery. I don't have many regrets in my life but I do regret not taking advantage of that offer. What an honor that would have been.

As a retirement gift, these guys gave me an American flag that had been flown in several different fighter aircraft. On the display, a plaque stated what kind of aircraft it had been on including a Russian Mig. It is by far one of the most precious gifts I have ever been given.

They all still come to Alaska every year and fish with different fishing charters. When they're here, we try to make it a point to visit them. They are great guys, good friends and we all met through fishing. Crazy!

## Dave and the Minnesota Gang

Dave Droen was a retired DC 10 captain for Northwest Airlines and lived in Minneapolis. I took him fishing my second year in business, and there began the NW Airline connection. Within a few years, it seemed like I was taking half of all their pilots and flight attendants on fishing charters. Minnesota became my number two state next to California from where my clients came from.

We became such good friends with these people that when one of the flight attendants we knew retired, Northwest offered her and her family a free trip anywhere in the world where they fly as a retirement gift.

They chose to come to Alaska in the middle of winter to spend a week with Dawn and I and do some ice fishing and spend some time at our cabin. All I can say is that it's nice to have friends that like you that much to do that. It's pretty cool.

There names were Bill and Linda. They made several trips to Alaska to be with us, and always brought some of their family along. They loved the Kasilof River. I just learned while I was writing this book that Bill had died of a liver disease. I hear the family wants to bring some of his ashes up here to be put at our Kasilof River property. I was really happy to hear that they want to do this. He was a really cool guy.

Now Dave would come to Alaska three or four times a year to fish with me, and each time he came, he would bring me a case of prime porterhouse steaks and a burlap sack full of freshly picked corn on the cob.

For probably the next fifteen years I never bought a steak, and I ate steak all the time. As for the corn, not many people in Alaska can say they eating one day old fresh picked corn on the cob. Life is good.

One day I was looking through some old Alaska magazines and saw an advertisement from Northwest airlines. It was a full page ad about flying on their new spacious DC 10 aircraft with a direct flight from Minneapolis to Anchorage. I cut it out and sent it to Dave as he was one of the original DC 10 captains that flew that route.

A few years later Dawn and I took a trip down to Minnesota and spent a night at Dave's house. On his wall was that advertisement all framed up nice and neat. It was pretty cool that I was able to give him something special besides a fishing trip. Dave died a few years back, but we remain in contact with many of our Minnesota friends.

Bill and Linda with there first fish they ever caught with me. Matt my deckhand is standing next to Linda.

## The Canadians

Here's another fun bunch. Just like the fighter pilots, these guys were here to fish, drink beer and have fun. They owned a bunch of land in Alberta with world class whitetail hunting on it. They always offered me to come down and hunt with them.

A few years went by and another friend of mine Bernie, who was also my taxidermist, had just returned home from a guided hunt in Alberta. I believe he said he paid about two thousand dollars for the hunt. I told him that I could go to Alberta anytime I wanted to and hunt for free. Bernie did everything but beg me to set up a hunt and take him. I called my friends in Canada, and the trip was on.

The following November Bernie and I flew to Alberta. When we arrived in Calgary there was my friend Terry Vockeroth at the gate holding up a sign with our names on it like we were someone important. If you knew Terry, you would appreciate it as he was kind of a screwball.

We go to Terry's farm which is out in the middle of nowhere just to find out that we're going back to Calgary the next day for an NHL hockey game. This was news to me. When we get to the game, there was another surprise waiting for us. Terry has us set up in a private executive booth.

So here we are watching the New York Rangers play the Calgary Flames, eating shrimp and drinking beer. Now, this is my kind of deer hunt. The only bad part of the game was we ran out of shrimp half way through the third period. I just thought how in the heck am I going to tell Dawn this one.

A few days later Terry and his wife Peggy take us to meet his brother and sister-in-law Wayne and Jackie, and have dinner with them. The dinner table was full of food. Jackie tells us that she knows its Thanksgiving Day in the USA and she wanted to make us something special.

Bernie and I had totally forgotten it was Thanksgiving since we were there to hunt. What hospitality! We were probably the only people in Canada that night eating a Thanksgiving dinner. I will never forget it.

Wayne died a few years back and is missed. He was a really cool guy. Terry still comes to Alaska every year with a group of people, and when he's here, we make it a point to get together for a beer and a laugh. He even brought me a badger one year. I will talk about that later.

Wayne with a nice Alberta whitetail deer.

## A.C. the Dentist

Ace was a dentist from Olympia who I met early on in my career. I met Ace through his brother George who sold me my place on the Kenai. The first time I took Ace fishing his bill was twelve hundred dollars. He told me he could pay that or if I would like he would start a retirement account for me with Fidelity and put two thousand dollars in it. I accepted, thank god.

At that time, I didn't have front teeth. Over the years this would drive Ace nuts. One year Dawn and I took a trip to Seattle for a Seahawks game and invited Ace to join us, which he did. Apparently, he had plans for me after the game that I knew nothing about. When the game was over Ace tells me, I'm going with him. He says he just wants to look over my teeth. Dawn was already in on this plan.

When we get to his office at about six o'clock on a Sunday evening, and I see one of his nurses there at the chair waiting, I knew something was up. All I know is that by ten o'clock I believe I had six root canals done. The next day I was back in a chair again at a different dentist office getting a bridge made. What would normally take a few weeks I was getting done in a few hours.

All I could think about was this was going to be the most expensive football game I ever went to. Ace tells me all these other dentists want is a fishing trip to Alaska. The following year I took all these dentists fishing, and the funny thing was, they still paid me for it. Amazing!

For the next several years I took Ace and his buddy's fishing. He always told me if I ever needed to borrow money he would loan me some. Now I hate borrowing money from anyone, but one year I took advantage of it and asked Ace if I could borrow twenty-five thousand dollars for a boat that I wanted. Ace pulled out his checkbook and wrote me the check on a handshake. Again, totally amazing!

Two weeks later I sold one of my boats and paid Ace back ten thousand dollars. I told him I would pay five thousand a year for the next three years to pay the loan off. Ace then asks me how much fifteen thousand dollars' worth of fishing would buy, which is obviously a lot of fishing. He then gives me no choice; he is going to buy fifteen thousand dollars' worth of fishing, and I am to put five thousand a year away in the retirement account that he started for me years earlier, which is just what I did. What kindness and generosity, and just to think it all started with a day of fishing.

I want to share one funny fishing story with Ace. One year he brought his son David up to fish as a graduation gift. David was reading all my NRA stickers on my truck and asks what the ILA stands for. I tell him it's just another branch of the NRA and I hear him tell Ace that he is going to join the NRA when he gets his first gun. That just got my attention.

When we got back to my house, I was showing David all my guns. The last one I pulled out of the gun safe was a Chinese SKS assault rifle. I handed it to him and told him congratulations on graduating from high school and all I ask is that you join the NRA. You would have thought I gave him a million dollars.

The next day Ace comes up to me and says thanks a lot, his mother is going to totally freak out when he gets home with an assault rifle. It was the first gun in the family.

Several years later, long after I was done fishing, I get a call from David. He was in Alaska and wanted to stop by and see me. When he gets to my house the first words he tells me is "thanks a lot for giving me that gun." He then pulls out his phone and starts showing me pictures of all the machine guns he builds. He became a gun lunatic. I laugh every time I think about it. At least I inspired someone in my life. Ha!

## Matt my deckhand

When I started taking my friend Jonathan Blattmachr fishing I eventually got to know his entire family, which seemed to be common with a lot of the people I took fishing. Jonathan lived in New York and his brother Doug and his family lived in Anchorage and had a place in Sterling on the Kenai River just down river from us. Matt was Jonathon's nephew.

When Matt Blattmachr was fourteen he kept bugging me to be a deckhand, which I never had before. I used to do all the work myself. I figured this was going to be a pain in the ass, but I said ok. I also told his parents that he is probably going to see and hear things that you might not want a fourteen year old kid to hear and see. They figured he was going to see the real world sooner or later so he had might as well do it.

Matts first day on the job was the craziest day of Halibut fishing I ever had. I normally shoot any Halibut over eighty pounds. That day we had four shooters with the largest fish weighing two hundred and sixty five pounds. It was unbelievable! Man, did we ever have our work cut out for us. Matt loved it and I was thankful he was there.

265 pound Halibut on Matt's first day.

All my tip money that I use to get was now going to Matt, and he was raking it in. All my clients really liked him. You don't meet many fourteen or fifteen year old kids that can sit in a boat and hold an intelligent conversation with strangers. It was truly one of the smarter decisions I made in the fishing business, and when he got his drivers license, I now had a designated driver so I could enjoy a cold beer on the way home from fishing.

When Matt was sixteen he got his pilots license. This is how crazy smart this kid is and he choose to be my deckhand out of all things. When he was eighteen he got his marine captains license and started taking my clients in his boat. Many days we would have both boats out on the water fishing side by side. We had a blast.

My fighter pilot clients were going to try to help get him accepted into the Air Force Academy so he could become a fighter pilot, which was Matt's dream. There was one small problem. Matt's eyes weren't perfect, and if you have anything wrong with you the Air Force is not going to teach you how to fly fighter jets for obvious reasons. All the fighter pilots really liked Matt.

When Matt was twenty three he married his high school sweetheart Emily. Dawn and I attended their wedding. I was so proud to know that

I was part of his life and he was part of mine. He was the kind of kid that just gave you faith in humanity.

Matt now runs their family business in Anchorage and is doing very well for himself. Just last summer, Matt and Emily flew their plane down from Anchorage to Homer to Halibut fish with me and his uncle Jonathon. When the fishing was over and it was time to go back to the plane for the trip home to Anchorage, I just thought to myself how lucky I was to have ever gotten to know such an incredible young man. We remain close friends and I look forward to fishing with him again. Damn, is life ever amazing or what.

I could probably write ten books of cool story's that I had with people I took fishing. I took people fishing from all over the USA, Canada, Europe and people from right here in Alaska. In fact, one-quarter of my business came from Anchorage. There were doctors, attorneys, oil executives, politicians such as George Sullivan and Tom Fink just to name a few, and just regular working people trying to get by in life.

If I needed an attorney, I had the best pit bull lawyer money could buy. In fact, I believe I was the only sport fishing charter business on the Kenai Peninsula that received an Exxon settlement check from the oil spill. If I needed a doctor, it was no problem. If I wanted Seahawk football tickets, no problem. Dawn and I went to Seattle for many years to watch football and never bought a ticket. This was back when people in Seattle couldn't even get tickets. It was awesome. All I had to do was take these people fishing.

The perks and the friendships that were made through the fishing business were priceless. I could not have been more thankful, but the fact was, I was done. Life goes on!

## CHAPTER 15

# Building our next house

Dawn and I with a Yelloweye limit, also known as red snapper from Prince William Sound

Dawn with fresh crab. Notice the name of the boat in the background.

My first summer of retirement Dawn and I started exploring Prince William Sound. Things I couldn't do when I had to fish for a living. I would like to say it is one of the most beautiful places in Alaska, but then the whole state is beautiful.

We also started looking at remote property in interior Alaska. We really wanted to find a place in Paxson. We went there for many years in the winter and fell in love with it. The fishing and hunting up in that country was great. The people that live up in that part of Alaska are just good people. They're the kind of people you expect to meet in Alaska. There was nothing in that area for sale that appealed to us.

Every time we came home from these trips, we would go to our cabin and hang out for a few days. One day while we were at the cabin, it hit us.

We have been looking for paradise all over Alaska, and it was right under our feet. We already owned it.

In 2005, we decided to sell our house in Sterling and build a house on the river and live happily ever after off the grid. It sounded good to me. To do this, we would have to find another piece of property on the road system as close as possible to the river property for a staging area. I could build a small place there, and we would have a place to park our boats, snow machines and everything else we owned. Sounded good to me!

Selling our Sterling house was easier than we planned. The first person that looked at it, three weeks after we listed it made an offer we couldn't refuse. Let's just say I tripled my money, but we had only 10 days to move.

We had good friends in Sterling, Jim and Debbie Bass who owned a liquor store with an apartment above it which they rented to us for the winter. I felt like a junky living upstairs from the dealer being that close to a liquor store. Dawn would stay in Sterling and work her business, and I would stay at our River property and finish our river house which was now framed up. It was all systems go.

When spring came, it was time to move to our new Kasilof property on the road system and build another house. A small house, yeah right! Once I had the land cleared, and the hole dug for the foundation we pitched a tent and moved in. From May until September we lived in a tent. Not bad for a couple of fifty-year-olds.

Now, this house was supposed to be small as we were going to live up at the river. The outfit that did our excavation work convinced me to go two stories for resale value as we do have a good mountain view. After all, I just made a killing of our last house, tax-free at that.

So now we have a two story, two baths and three-bedroom house with a two-car attached garage for just Dawn and I and I'm really glad we did it. We do have an awesome view of the mountains with wilderness as far as the eye can see and we're in a great neighborhood with good neighbors. So much for the resale value, it's not for sale and so much for living up at the river. Damn, oh well, life is good.

A few years after this, Dawn sold her business Toner Resource, which she owned for eighteen years and started a new one, OMG Services. The omg stands for office machine girl. She did this all on her own, and I couldn't be prouder of her. I ended up getting a part-time job and became a Zamboni driver out of all crazy things. It was my first job in over twenty years.

We continue to go to Prince William Sound, and yes, I do spend lots of time up at the river house enjoying the peace and beauty of this great state. I spent the winter up at the river writing this book. All I did was write, read and feed eagles. It was also during this time frame when I first really started to realize just how well Alaska treated me. I do not think there is any other state in our great nation that I could of pulled this off. Crazy!

CHAPTER 16

# Hunting

For all the years that I guided, I could never go moose hunting as I had to fish all through the fall season. However, my rifle was always in the boat. One year I was fishing on the upper Kasilof river with some good clients from Minnesota when a spike bull comes out on the bank.

I brought the boat up to it, confirmed it was a spike and told my clients "cover your ears boys." When I shot the moose, my clients all pulled out their phones and started calling all their friends telling them "you're not going to believe this, our guide just shot a moose." It was pretty cool.

After I gutted the moose, I continued down river and got my clients their limit of fish. We then went back to my place and processed the fish. After this, I got a friend of mine and went back up the river and butchered the moose and made it back home by five o'clock. Not a bad day's work. That was the only moose I shot during all the years I guided.

However, during this time, I did make it to Kodiak Island sixteen years straight for deer hunting. The season was five months long, and November was the best hunting, long after fishing season was over. And Kodiak has some of the best deer hunting in the world.

A few nice Kodiak deer

A few deer from Prince William sound. Notice the pile of shrimp to go with the deer. Life is good.

Nothing like a few fresh crab to go with the deer

On my first trip there I met a man named Gary Ennen, who just so happened to be the head man of the National Weather Service for Kodiak and also owned a boat. A must for deer hunting! That was the beginning of a long friendship which continues today.

Throughout those years I shot eighty deer. That's not counting what other people shot that was with me. All I can say is that my freezers were full of some of the best eating meat Alaska has to offer. While I'm on this subject with Gary, I want to share one funny but dumb story. One year Dawn and I were going to fly to Kodiak to spend Thanksgiving with Gary and do a little hunting. This would be the first time I would fly there as I had always taken the state ferry Tustumena.

While we were waiting at our gate in Anchorage, they announce that there delaying the flight due to bad weather in Kodiak. Everyone at the gate just laughed and said, "yep that's Kodiak". It does have some of the worst weather in North America, let alone Alaska.

About thirty minutes later they announce that they're boarding the plane, the weather has improved in Kodiak. When we get in the air, the captain comes on the radio and says the ceiling is fifteen hundred feet and should be a nice flight in.

When we get there, the weather sucked. It was socked in and very turbulent. We missed our first approach and had to circle around for a second try. If they miss the second approach it's back to Anchorage we go. We did make it on the second try.

Gary meets us at the airport bar and tells me since he knew they wouldn't leave Anchorage until the ceiling was a certain altitude, he just simply raised it in his weather report to get the plane in the air. Thanks a lot, Gary. It scared the shit out of me. All I know is that I would never fly back to Kodiak. I will take the state ferry in thirty-foot seas any day.

Now that I'm retired from fishing, let the moose hunting begin. I and my main fishing and hunting partner Gene Dyson, were ice fishing the winter before I retired and not only found a great place to fish but also an area where we figured could have some good moose hunting. Man did we ever.

Just a few of the moose we have shot. The freezers are full

Now, this area is inside the Kenai National Wildlife Refuge where the poor little redneck hunters can't hunt because they can't use there four wheelers, thank god. We have taken twelve bulls in the last fourteen years out of this area, most of them trophy size bulls, and we're not even trophy hunters; we're meat hunters.

While I am on the subject of meat hunting, I want to share one really cool story. I was moose hunting at the Mullican family homestead not long before I moved out there. All their family members are meat hunters. No one cares who shoots it as long as someone gets one. At that time I had never shot a moose before. We all split up and sure as hell I come into two bulls. No one talked about this. I figured screw it, I shot them both. After I gutted them out I hiked back to there house to get help. They had all heard the gun shots and were there waiting for me to congratulate me on my first moose and asked me how big it was. I took off my pack and pulled out two hearts and livers and said "you mean how big were they". It was pretty cool. Man did we ever have some meat that year.

As I say this, I want you to know that if wild game didn't taste so good, you would never see me out hunting. You would also never see me join a group like the Safari Club. What a bunch of phony people. My love is for fishing, not hunting. It's much more enjoyable and a whole lot less work. However, my freezers are usually full of really good food. Life is damn good.

One last story about hunting! I love a good prank as you can tell by now. My friend Gary was going to come over from Kodiak one winter to do some ptarmigan hunting with me and damn if I didn't get picked for federal jury duty for that month which means I would have to go to Anchorage if they called me.

Right when Gary arrived sure as hell, they call my group. Now I had a decision to make, abide by the law and go to jury duty or go bird hunting. I chose to hunt. It didn't seem like that big of a deal.

A few weeks later I was telling my good friend and attorney, Dennis about skipping out on jury duty. He tells me "man you can't do that, that's a big time no-no" and I told him to screw that, I did it and they're not going to do nothing.

A few days later Dennis calls my friend George, and disguise's his voice and says he's an officer from the federal court looking for me. George calls me up and asks me if I'm in any kind of trouble. I told him no that the only thing I have done was skip out of jury duty. George tells me that there's an officer of the courts looking for me and I might want to call the federal courthouse. Just great, this is all I need.

So, I called the courthouse and told the lady that I understand that there looking for me and she says." nope we're not looking for you and then she sees that I skipped out of jury duty and tears into my ass. She tells me if they call any group, I was to be there with a letter explaining why I missed jury duty. I had to have George make me an official letter saying why I wasn't there. I turned myself in when I didn't have to thanks to my good friend Dennis. Man, he got me bad on that one. I deserved it.

CHAPTER 17

# THE BADGER

One of my favorite things about fishing and life, in general, is pulling a good prank on someone. If it creates laughter, I'm all for it. When I first started building my cabins on the Kasilof River property, I needed to find a staging area to work from as all my building material was going to be snow machined in.

I had heard about a man named Larry Meyers, who had a homestead about three and a half miles from my property on the road system. I was told that Larry was a retired hunting guide and commercial fisherman and likes good food. I went to the local butcher and told him to make me some of the biggest porterhouse steaks he could make. I needed Larry a whole lot more than he needed me.

I went to his homestead, introduced myself and handed him a bag of steaks and asked if I could use his homestead as a staging area. He invites me in for coffee, and we immediately became friends. He had dead animals all over his house, just like mine. He has hunted and trapped for just about everything there was to hunt for in Alaska, and he was also a prankster.

Over the years we remained good friends. Larry always kept a spot plowed out for me to park my truck and trailer. When I moved to Kasilof, I no longer needed Larry's homestead as I was now snow machining to the cabin from my house, but I always made it a point to stop in and visit

Larry. The coffee was always on, and there was usually a good story or joke to hear about a prank he pulled on someone.

My friends from Canada called me and said they were coming up to Alaska and asked if I wanted a Badger. I presumed it was a Badger hide or a mounted Badger since I have all sorts of dead stuff on my walls. They brought me a whole frozen Badger. I guess the customs guy couldn't believe it. They said they never saw anything like that come through before.

So now I got this frozen Badger. I threw it in the freezer and the following winter Dawn, and I thawed it out and took it to our cabin to skin it. Larry is going to snow machine in and have dinner with us that night. This is where it gets good.

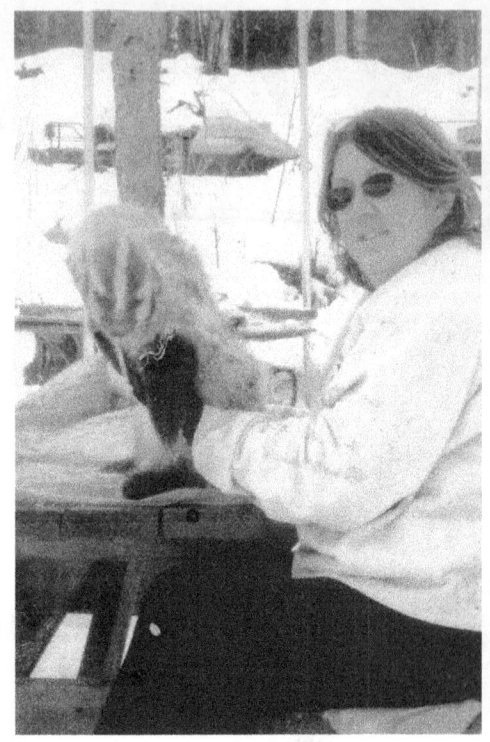

Dawn with the badger

After she skinned it, I was looking at the carcass hanging on the pole and thought, this could be something. I called Larry and asked him if there were any badgers in Alaska, which there's not, and he answers back "hell no there's no Badgers in Alaska." I told him I just shot one out on the river and he tells me I'm full of crap.

When he comes riding in, he sees the carcass hanging on the pole and sees the hide he says, "it is a Badger." Throughout the whole dinner, the Badger was the main conversation. How did the Badger get here? Was it some one's pet? Who would have a pet Badger? It was everything Dawn and I could do to hold a straight face.

Now Larry couldn't keep a secret from anyone, so I told him whatever you do don't tell anyone about this. As soon as Larry left, I called one of his best friends Robbie, who's a real trapper and had been burned by Larry before with his pranks and asked if he wanted in on this one. He tells me he would pay to get in on this.

As soon as Larry got home, he called Robbie and told him the story. We waited for about a week and had another friend call Larry and tell him "you're not going to believe this; you know how Lesterson got a Badger up at the river, Robbie got one yesterday in his trap line." They called me and said he took the bait again.

I called Larry and told him I was going to be snow machining to the cabin and I was going to swing in and pay a visit. I then told him "whatever you do don't tell anyone about the Badger. I called fish and game, and they confiscated the Badger. It's a federal law to kill a Badger in Alaska, and I had to get a lawyer". The phone went silent. Larry then says, "I wonder what happens if someone traps one."

Then Robbie and I planned to meet at Larry's at a certain time. He would give me a five-minute jump. When I got to Larry's the first thing he asks me is "are you really in trouble?", and I tell him "big trouble." He then tells me "you're not going to believe this; Robbie got one in his trap line." Oh my god was it hard to hold a straight face.

About that time Robbie is knocking on the door. Larry looks at me and asks me to tell Robbie about the badger. I told him, "I'm not saying anything". He then asks Robbie to tell me about the badger. Robbie then says he got a Badger in his trap line the other day, and I told him that I got one up at the river last week. Larry then jumps up and says, "what the hell is going on with all these Badgers." When he found out he got burned by both of us, he couldn't believe it. The king of pranks got pranked. His nickname became Badger Meyers, and his friends would tell him to stop badgering them. Larry took it well and laughed about it with the rest of us. Larry died a few years ago and is truly missed. He was a really cool and fun-loving guy who enjoyed a good laugh. He was my kind of person.

CHAPTER 18

# MY THOUGHTS AND OPINIONS

### The Kenai National Wildlife Refuge

When President Carter changed the Kenai National Moose Range to a wildlife refuge and expanded the National Park system across Alaska, I despised it just like many Alaskans did. My view was that this was more Federal overreach into states' rights.

There was a big protest up by Denali Park called the great Denali Trespass. There were probably a few thousand people there, mostly from Fairbanks. People were shooting ptarmigan, riding snow machines and other things that were now illegal in the newly expanded park. The State Troopers were there to keep the peace, and no Feds were to be seen. I was one of these protesters.

I didn't vote for Carter and couldn't stand his political views, but now forty-two years later with all the changes that I have seen on the Kenai Peninsula and Alaska, all I can say is thank you, President Carter. With the redneck mentality that I have seen on the Kenai Peninsula, I have no doubt in my mind that if it weren't for the refuge, you would see nothing but four-wheeler trails, roads, logging, etc. across the whole Peninsula.

The oil industry brought a lot of wealth to Alaska and improved the quality of life, but it also brought a lot of trashy redneck people with it that would rather develop every square inch of this state and make it just like the one they came from. The most common bumper sticker in Fairbanks at the end of the Trans-Alaska Pipeline construction was (Happiness is watching ten thousand Texans leave Alaska with an Okie under each arm).

I have known people that have lived here for twenty years that never knew you couldn't use a four-wheeler on the Refuge which told me they never really got out and enjoyed the hunting and fishing. It's their loss.

The really cool thing with the Refuge is that there is something for most user groups. There are areas open for snowmachine use when there's adequate snowfall, which I use to get to my cabin on the Kasilof River. The Refuge also has areas that are non-motorized use only, which I use often. Four wheelers are permanently off limits on the Refuge which is fine with me, and I own one. Power boats are off limits above Skilak lake on the Kenai river. It is the only part of the Kenai river that I would even consider fishing again.

There are a couple of lakes on the refuge that Dawn and I fished at for many years. You had to walk back into these lakes, and through the years we never saw another human fishing them. There were no names to these lakes, so Dawn and I decided we wanted to name them John and Dawn lakes. We did a little homework on it and found out unless your name was John Kennedy or Ronald Regan, you weren't naming any lake inside the wilderness, and that was just fine with me.

Where else in North America can you go ice fishing on a lake full of fish and not see another human? If it wasn't for hearing an airplane flying by from time to time, you would think you're the only human on earth. I can hardly wait to take my grandkids ice fishing and let them experience just that, the sound of silence. It's priceless. The things I do on the Refuge are the very reasons I came to

A good day of shed hunting inside the refuge.

Alaska for in the first place. I'm just surprised at how many people don't appreciate it. In my opinion, the Refuge is what makes my river property valuable, because it's surrounded by it. Again, thank you, President Carter.

## Guiding

As you could tell, when I retired from fishing I didn't have much good to say about guides in general, especially Kenai River guides and I still don't for the most part. There are however, some good guides out there and there are just enough bad ones to give them all a bad name. When I quite fishing, I was almost embarrassed to tell anyone what I did for a living.

In the summer when I watch the guides go by there are some that remind me of myself when I was getting started. They are loving their job being on the river, and their clients are having fun. Then there are guides who go by that I feel sorry for their clients. There no more a guide than I am an astronaut. Unfortunately, there are plenty of them like that.

I had some clients of mine who were lawyers go out with a long-time guide on the Kenai River who is still a guide today. They caught twelve silvers with him and had a good time with him until the trip was over. They asked about cleaning the fish. The guide told them he could do it for five bucks a fish. They took their fish with them. That extra sixty bucks the guide tried to get, cost him several thousand dollars in lost business. What a fool. These are the guides that have no repeat business.

Even in the Halibut charter industry, I could see the stupidity in what some of the charters were doing. When charters start advertising, leave the harbor in the evening and return in the early morning so their clients could get two limits of fish, you could see the writing on the wall. It didn't take long to get that provision shutdown and for a good reason.

I try to tell anyone that is going to a sport and recreation trade show to find a charter service, that you are looking to get screwed. Ask the guide service how long they have been in business. If the answer is more than two years and they have fancy brochures to lure you in, let the buyers' beware. Your clients are your best advertisers. Man did I ever learn that in a big way.

Now as I say this, I want to say that I was proud to be part of this industry. I made a good living and of course made a lot of friends and priceless memories. I just wish the state would have limited the number of guides many years ago. None of this would have ever been a problem. All I know is that I did it right and I'm proud of it.

## Feeding wildlife

Over the years I have spent a small fortune feeding animals and love doing it. In Alaska, it is illegal to feed moose. In the city it is understandable but if you live out in the country and it's a bad winter with deep snow, I am going to feed them. I'm not going to sit back and watch a moose die of starvation if I can help it. Screw the law.

Back in the 90s there was a really hard winter and the moose were dropping like flies. There were a lot of dead moose that year. We had one show up in my yard all skin and bones and could barely walk. I went to the feed store and bought a bale of alfalfa. It didn't take the moose long to start feeding on it. I would only give her a little at a time along with willow and birch brows. We named this moose Little Bud.

After a few weeks Little Bud trusted me enough to let me hand feed her. She would follow me all around outside the house and she would sleep near our dogs when they were outside. All my neighbors were coming over to let there kids watch the moose and

Our dogs always slept with little bud.

feed her. We did this all winter. When spring came we sent her on her way to go be a moose. It was very rewarding.

The following winter was a much easier winter. In December Little Bud shows back up and I figured ,what the heck, I'm going to feed her again. It took her five days this time to trust me enough to take it from my hands. I did this all winter again and this time Dawn was giving me a hard time about it because it was an easy winter and I was spending a hundred bucks a month on feed. I had become too attached to her. She was my personal moose.

Feeding time on the back porch.

The next winter it was even an easier year. There was hardly any snow on the ground and I figured I would never see her again. In February Dawn looks out the window and tells me there's a moose by our porch and it looks like Little Bud. I ran out on the porch and called her name and she walked right up to me and let me pet her. Dawn comes running up to me and gives me some money and tells me to hurry up and get to the feed store before she leaves. Dawn was as happy to see Little Bud back as I was. All I know is that I saved that moose's life a few years ago and had fun doing it.

In the last few years at the cabin, I have been feeding salmon carcuses to the eagles on the Kasilof River. They are getting really use to me feeding them. I checked in with the state and the feds to make sure it was legal and it is, as long as you don't harm one. My goal was to have one land on me and hand feed it and film it with my Go-Pro and post it on You tube. I came close. Now the story is going to get good.

My neighbor Ben, who has property down river from me has the bright idea to put the camera out on the ice and put fish right in front of it and we would film them coming in right at it. It worked great and we made some really cool videos. Then he has the bright idea to put a piece

The camera thief

of fish on top of the camera and really get a close up. The eagle came in and not only took the fish it took the camera with it and flew across the river to a tree branch and dropped it. Ben had to snow machine across the river to get to where the tree was and got the camera back with some incredible footage. Now the story gets even better.

We get the brilliant idea to put a floatable handle on the camera, set the piece of fish on the handle so we could get some good aerial footage. We thought whatever tree it would land in and drop the camera, we would just go get it. It worked just like we planned on except for one thing. Instead of going to a tree branch to land in like they have done all winter, the eagle took the camera to its nest high in a tree hanging out over a bluff. From the bottom of the tree, Ben was able to download the video to his phone. We lost a $350.00 dollar camera that day but got a million dollar video out of it.

The fact is I love to feed animals. I hand feed grey jays all the time here at my cabin. On bad years I cut down birch trees for the moose. I will always continue to help wildlife out when there is a need . I think it is the very least a person could do.

## Sex, Drugs and Rock and Roll

Ah yes, some of my favorite things to talk about besides fishing. My life could be described in two parts, BD and AD. Before Dawn and After Dawn, with the latter obviously being the best.

The 70s and 80s were a wild and crazy time. When I got out of the US Army, Fairbanks was rocking. The pipeline construction was just ending, and everyone had money. There were hookers on all the street corners wearing fur coats, the bars were all open until 5:00 am and there was one other thing that was plentiful, cocaine.

When I wasn't fishing, you could usually find me at one of the bars snorting coke and chasing girls. With no coke, you might as had well stay home or go buy a prostitute. Heck, I had more one-night stands than I ever had girlfriends. Until Dawn, the longest I ever had a girlfriend was four months.

I never bought a prostitute, but with all the money I spent on cocaine chasing girls, it would have been a lot cheaper. It was kind of a blur, but I have to say I really had fun. I just wish I could have all the money back that I spent on cocaine. I'm sure it would be in the tens of thousands of dollars. I'm not proud of any of this, and I'm not ashamed of it either, it's just the way it was. I wasn't the only one. I think I was in the majority. I'm just so thank full that I never hurt anyone.

The one thing I do know is that out of all the drugs I ever did, and it was lots, the only one that ever bit me was alcohol, the most legal one of them all. If cocaine was cheap and socially accepted like it is in Peru, I would probably start my day every day with a line of coke. I didn't see any harm in it besides the price. I still enjoy a pot brownie from time to time, and I enjoy a good drink, but that's it, no more drugs. Been there and done that and lived to tell about it.

While I'm on this subject, I want to share one funny story about marijuana. When I took my last trip to Montana, not long after I got out of the Army, my dad and I went on a three-day fishing trip. I was sitting out on a picnic table rolling a joint when my dad, who was in the camper, asks me what I was doing. I figured screw it, its time he knows. I tell him I'm rolling a joint.

He came walking up to me, and I handed it to him and said "why don't you light this up" since he smoked cigarettes anyway. I started to put my pot away, and he asks "aren't you going to smoke any" not knowing that you pass it back and forth. I didn't say a word and rolled myself one.

He smoked that whole joint, and we went back to fishing. I have never seen my dad laugh as hard as he did that day. Man did he ever get stoned. It was by far one of the most memorable days of fishing that I ever had with my dad. The next day while we're eating breakfast, my dad says to me "that stuff doesn't even give you a hangover." Four months later when my parents moved to Alaska, the first thing my dad did when they got to my house was to hand me a bag of pot and tells me to roll us one. I couldn't believe it. He smuggled a bag of pot through Canada back when it was still a serious crime. My dad went from Mr. Military drill sergeant to Chech and Chong right in front of my eyes. It was awesome. My poor mother!

I am happy that the state of Alaska along with many other states has finally legalized the retail sales of marijuana. Why make something illegal that can't be stopped? And besides that, it's a whole lot less harmful than alcohol and tobacco.

Now when it comes to meth and heroin, screw those guys. It is my opinion, when they catch a person cooking meth for resale or selling heroin laced with fetynal, they need to lock them up for life. Those drugs are ruining a lot of people's lives. Also, first responders need to quit carrying those Narcon kits that bring a person back from an overdose. They're the loser users that put the needle in their arm in the first place. Screw it, let them die.

And one last thing, I do love good old rock and roll. I love good music. In my life, I have had the pleasure to go to a Johnny Cash concert in San Antonio, a Merle Haggard concert in Denver, an Elvin Bishop concert and a Chuck Berry concert in Fairbanks and two Rolling Stones concerts, one in Las Vegas and one in Hawaii, and they were all a blast. Life is good.

### Colin Kaepernick and Fishing

As you can tell by now, I love the United States and Alaska with all my heart. There is no other place on the planet that I could have lived my life the way I did. The first time I watched the NFL football players kneel for the National Anthem, I wanted to puke. What a bunch of low life parasites. That must take a real high IQ to protest racial injustice that way. After reading the book *Freedom Writers Diary*, and what a low paid teacher could do to teach and mentor kids of all races from the inner city, and turn them into successful people, I feel even stronger about my opinion now more than ever. A teacher could do that and a millionaire football player can only take a knee for the anthem. Again, what a high IQ.

Dawn and I went to Seattle every year for many years to watch the Seattle Seahawks play. We were on the waiting list for many years for season tickets. One year we even went to the pro bowl in Hawaii. I use to go with my dad to mile high stadium for the Bronco games when I was a kid. In 2001 Dawn and I were going to the Super Bowl until 9/11 screwed things all up. Now I wouldn't go to a NFL game if it was free. I would however like to thank Colin Kaepernick for freeing up another day of the week for me to go fish.

Pro Bowl. Never again!

Every year our local hardware store has an ice fishing derby for the month of February. Last year I went in to sign up for the derby on the Friday before the Super Bowl. I told the employees that I was going to do something that I had never done before. I told them that for the first time in my life I was not going to watch the Super Bowl and that I was going to go fishing instead. They said, "good for you we're not watching it either". I also told them that as much as I hate to see other people when I am ice fishing, I hope I see people everywhere.

As I was driving out Swanson River Road to fish on Super Bowl Sunday there were cars parked at every trailhead. The lake I chose to fish had three different groups on it. After an hour or two one couple came and asked me how the fishing was. I told them that it wasn't that good and that the only reason I was out there was to protest something that was on TV at the current time. The guy walked up to me and shook my hand and said, "that is what they were doing also". I was proud. I know my dad would have been proud of me.

Alaska might be a long way from the lower 48 states but I swear people here love America more than most. There are more Veterans in Alaska per capita than any other state in the nation and when someone wants to show disrespect to our flag, they can kiss my proud American butt.

CHAPTER 19

## Conclusion

To sum it all up, I would have to say that my life has been a dream come true. Almost like a fantasy. Sure, there were sad times to go with the good, but that's life. I just wish it didn't go by so quickly. I guess the old saying, "time flies when you're having fun", is really true. Man did it ever fly by.

Some people think I'm lucky. I disagree. I earned everything I went after in life. No one gave me anything but a chance. I'm lucky I was born in the USA, the greatest country on earth, and I'm lucky I was raised by two loving parents but that's it, I earned everything else, and I'm proud of it. I truly lived the American dream. The same thing can be said about Dawn. No one gave her anything. She had the courage to quit her job and started her own business, and it worked.

The most valuable asset I have, I do not and cannot ever own. It's my friends. I'm not lucky to have the friends I have, blessed yes but not lucky. I earned them and what an asset they are. You truly can't have enough friends.

I have thought to myself if I had to live my life over again what I would do differently. The answer would probably have to be nothing. I would do it all over again the same way. It was way too much fun. I just wish my dad would have lived a little longer to watch me succeed in life and meet Dawn, but again that's life.

The two wisest things I ever did in my life were to drop out of high school and join the Army and get to Alaska and the second was to marry the first women I ever fell in love with, Dawn who is truly the love of my life.

So now here I am at the ripe old age of sixty, and I still haven't decided what I even want to do when I grow up. I guess I better hurry and think of something. The one thing I do know is I will spend the rest of my life in this great state and there will always be a fishing pole close by. Man did Alaska ever treat me good. I was truly blessed. Life is good.

Cheers.

www.ingramcontent.com/pod-product-compliance
Lightning Source LLC
Chambersburg PA
CBHW060841050426
42453CB00008B/776